The Progress
of the Seasons

"The great lawn of the field spread before us, as it spreads today. Pretty soon the announcer activated the public address system that until then I had heard only as background noise on the radio broadcasts of the games. It sounded quite different, more important and commanding, when you were actually there. 'Attention ladies and gentlemen. Here are the starting lineups for today's game.'"

The Progress

"Leading off, and playing
center field: DiMaggio.
DiMaggio, playing cen-
ter field."

GEORGE V. HIGGINS

Henry Holt and Company ♦ New York

of the Seasons

FORTY YEARS OF
BASEBALL
IN OUR TOWN

"Batting second, playing
shortstop: Pesky. Pesky,
playing shortstop."

LIBRARY OF CONGRESS CATALOGING-IN-PUBLICATION DATA
Higgins, George V., 1939–
The progress of the seasons.
1. Boston Red Sox (Baseball team) 2. Fenway Park
(Boston, Mass.) 3. Higgins, George V., 1939–
4. Authors, American—20th century—Biography.
I. Title
GV875.B62H46   1989   796.357′64′0974461   88-
34738
ISBN 0-8050-0913-2

Henry Holt books are available at special discounts for bulk
purchases for sales promotions, premiums, fund-raising, or
educational use. Special editions or book excerpts can also
be created to specification.

FOR DETAILS CONTACT:

Special Sales Director
Henry Holt and Company, Inc.
115 West 18th Street
New York, New York 10011

First Edition

Designed by Kathryn Parise
Printed in the United States of America
1   3   5   7   9   10   8   6   4   2

*Grateful acknowledgment is given for permission to use the
following photographs: endpaper photograph, courtesy of the
Boston Red Sox; photographs on pp. ii, iii, 36, 42, 56, 74,
154–55 (middle and right), courtesy of The Boston Globe;
photographs on pp. 9, 20–21, 31, 91, 110 (left), 111 (right),
154 (left), and 185, courtesy of the New England Sports Museum (photo on p. 9 by Robert Riger); photograph on p. 216,
courtesy of the Boston Public Library; photograph on pp. 110–
11 (middle), courtesy of Albie Walton.*

My mother, Doris Montgomery Higgins, has spent most of her life in houses and in cars, and in public places too, in the company of males who were almost always going to, coming from, watching, listening to, or arguing about baseball and the Red Sox—or complaining, in the off-seasons, that there wasn't any baseball. I heard her disparage this behavior and its subject only once, and I wasn't supposed to hear that.

So this book is for Doris, and it is about the men she loved and the baseball that she didn't, and she will say: "That figures," but she's earned it and it's hers—she's stuck with it, as she has been with us.

G. V. H.

The Progress
of the Seasons

"Batting third, and playing left field: Williams.
Williams, playing left field."

It was summertime, in 1946. I wore short pants and knee socks—this was an important day, although I do not have a photograph of it—and I probably wore a clip-on tie. My father parked the Studebaker at the gray stone station (it's gone now—first gutted by fire and then torn down), and we went into it and waited for the train. The newsstand sold the *Boston Post*, and Charlie most likely bought a copy. I was coming up on seven years old.

The train came. The passenger cars were dark green, and I remember vaguely that the interiors were sort of beige. If the seats were as high as I remember them (and they were), my feet did not touch the floor, so I probably curled my legs up under myself. I do remember that the seats were plush and so arranged that there were two facing two on each side of the aisle. Since there were three of us, we occupied one of the rows, most likely (again, as I remember it) on the left side of the train. We went through the Weymouths and the other towns until we came to South Station in Boston. We got off the train and got on a trolley car. You must understand now that I was a very small boy, and I did not know much of anything, so all of this was magic to me.

We took the trolley car to Kenmore Square. The trolley car was orange and green, with a yellow stripe, I think. We got off the trolley car and walked southwest on Brookline Avenue until we came to a brick edifice that had an etched gray cement sign on the front saying: FENWAY PARK. We went inside. It was comparatively dark, and there were a lot of people around. My father had the small pasteboard cards that enabled us to enter. Charlie went first, then John, with me. I did not let go of my father's hand. We bought some things that Charlie and John seemed to think we needed, and then we went along—they knew where we were going, and I always, rightly, trusted them, because they were good men; even little boys know that—to the proper place for us, and we emerged into the sunshine, at Section 17. If God is good—and I have been, pretty good, at least—when I die, St. Peter at the Pearly Gate will direct me down the ramp, then up the ramp, to Section 17, and John and Charlie will be sitting there, wondering why I'm late.

We went up to our seats and took them, the great lawn of the field spread before us as it spreads today. Pretty soon the announcer activated the public address system that until then I had heard only as background noise on the radio broadcasts of the games. It sounded quite different, more important and commanding, when you actually were there. "Attention, ladies and gentlemen. Here are the starting lineups for today's game."

That was the ceremonial beginning of more than forty years, so far, of following the Boston Red Sox, and trying to understand other complicated things as well. Some of those were games that were never played in sunshine, and could not have stood the light. No cheers were provoked when they happened, nor gladness warranted. They were not, like

2

baseball, lasting gifts to be carried with me carefully down the years, carefully kept from rust and moths in the winter months, unwrapped with happy gratitude when spring came to our town again. But baseball and the Red Sox, as much as they and I have changed, have sturdily remained, reliable and plain, nine young men on a level field, with bats and gloves and ball, an orderly and gracious world of bad tempers and foul language, precise rules and near riots, celebrations capped by requiems—and then we say: it's just a game. Maybe that is so in other towns I don't know well, but in Boston and at Fenway, it's a good deal more than that. It isn't only baseball that has its Opening Days; lives and memories have them too.

I do not remember the '38 maroon DeSoto coupe that my father drove the forty miles each way between our home in Rockland and his job teaching English at Natick High School. I know the car was bracketed by falling trees as he fought his way home through the disastrous hurricane that hit New England the year that it was new, and there are pictures of me in my mother's arms beside it, but John believed that no car was trustworthy after three years of steady service and traded it on the blue and gray '41 DeSoto coupe before I was two years old, long before my memory developed. There are pictures of the two of us with that car as background, too, but because the leaders of the world intervened in my father's orderly practices of acquisition and de-acquisition, I remember that one myself.

I remember lots of things, some of them certainly not the ones that my parents and grandparents wished me to record and cherish all my life. And the ones that they intended me to keep, I hold in a trust different from the motive of the gifts. The Christmases, for example: my grandfather, Charlie, and my father were determined that I should retain unsullied for as long as possible the mistaken belief that Santa Claus not only brought the plunder, but indeed the tree as well, and delayed his visits to the homes of other fitfully sleeping children, where he merely paused to drop off presents, in order that he might personally decorate our pine. I believed that Saint Nicholas rendered this extra service to me because I was special, you see, and I believed that because when I asked John and Charlie why the other kids already had their Christmas trees, days before we did, they told me that was the reason. I had not then developed much power of observation, and less still of deduction; it did not occur to me that there must be some explanation for the Christmas afternoon fatigue of a father and a grandfather of a small boy renitent against approaching sleep on Christmas Eve until around eleven o'clock. The presents and the tree were what they desired me to remember, and I do, but what sticks out now is how that tree and those gifts came to me.

There was then, I suppose, at least as much damned foolishness going around about the pain and deprivation of being an only child as there is today, but my father had been one himself, and he knew it for the buncombe it was. Being the only child in the third living generation of my small family was a gift of some obvious magnitude, especially in my early childhood years. (Later on, and not much later, either, the burdens of that status were made plain to me—I think the occasion most likely was when I brought home my first paper on which I received a B-minus from Miss Lannin's first grade and was kindly but firmly instructed, shortly before my fifth birthday, in 1944, that it was not acceptable. When Miss Lannin forbade me to write with my left hand, I knew better than to argue with her; I used my right.) Those memories of Christmases are not discrete in my memory today, as they were, each of them, meant to be by their creators; all the Christmases are jumbled up together in one corner of the mind's attic, a recipe for a pudding that was glorious, to be sure—not because it was memorable for each serving, but because it is to be treasured for all of them, and what they meant in continuity.

Early in the fall, usually in the first half of October, it begins to get cold and dark, windy and grim, in preparation for Christmas in New England. Then the snow comes, and the cold settles in, and the damned winter begins. I know each of us of a certain age believes that the winters came earlier when we were children, chilled more deeply with more snow, and lasted a lot longer (and the weather bureau records, oddly enough, tend to bear us out on that), but the winters of my childhood, I am grateful to say, were much bleaker than the winters that my daughter, Susan, and my son, John, had to endure to earn Christmas.

It was not because of the weather; it was because of little things that I most likely would not have noticed if my father and my mother had not called my attention to them. My father disliked the only spread available for his morning toast, and he complained about it every day. My mother made it by combining a relatively large amount of white grease with a smaller amount of yellow stuff, and squeezing it in a waxed-paper tube to mix it. She said it was margarine; he fumed that it was not butter. She said butter was not available, as he very well knew. This did not console him, nor did it improve his opinion of the heavily chickoried brown beverage she had to serve in place of coffee. Charlie's wife, John's mother, the forbidding and tyrannical Annie, was vastly overweight, ill-tempered, and lazy. Her only pleasure, aside from hectoring all who wandered within earshot of her favorite chair by the window, where she spent her days gobbling hard candies and spying on the neighbors' comings-in and goings-out, was the family's interminable Sunday drive in Charlie's '38 black Studebaker President sedan; she had to be denied that pleasure, most Sundays, because gasoline was rationed, and so were tires (the few available were made of something called synthetic rubber), and that did not sweeten her disposition. My mother occasionally burned her hands and forearms when the hot fat left by cooked meats spattered as she poured it from the skillet or the broiling pan into the used lard can, but she had to save that fat and turn it in at the store when we needed soap or lard. We had a little cocker spaniel, Blackie, and she got sick, but we couldn't take her to the veterinarian because the doctor had been drafted, whatever that meant; she spent her last night in a distempered fit, thrashing madly about the kitchen and crashing into things, and then she died. In the evenings John, feeling silly—and saying so—went out wearing a helmet and carrying a flashlight, to make sure the Nileses and the Smiths across the street, and the Lelyvelds next door to them, and the Hickeys and the Spences and the Ryans, too, for that matter, had their shades down tight and no light escaping. My friend Jack Metivier had an older brother, Joe, who was shot down when the B-17 he was piloting ran afoul of enemy defenses, but he was all right; I don't think the thought ever crossed my mind that I was very lucky indeed that John was too old and too out of shape to be drafted.

I was fifteen when Charlie died in 1955, and John handled matters with sad, proud bravery; I think when John died, in 1966, I was able to do my part, at the age of twenty-six, chiefly because one numb corner of my mind kept transmitting the comforting though deceitful message that I was only called upon for interim management duties until John got back from wherever he was to resume his charge of things. After all, his maroon 98 Oldsmobile Holiday coupe was right out there in the garage, four years old and more than ready, in his estimation, to be traded on a new one. His Doberman—I had bought Abby when our German shepherd, Pache, died, but Abby was John's dog, rising up on her hind legs to place both front paws on his shoulders and lick his face when he came home—was still, though puzzled, looking for him through the house. He had died in my hands in the hospital, having used one of his last breaths to tell me I had been "a pretty good boy," but that didn't mean he was gone; he couldn't be, because I owed him an equal crack of faint praise—"And you've been a reasonably decent father"? Perhaps. Something along that line, at least; John had no respect for anyone who took a sly dig without responding. I shook the hands of the people who came to the house between two and four in the afternoon, and seven and nine in the evening, and when the last of the stragglers had decamped around ten-thirty or so, at Doris's direction I sat down in his chair at the head of the table, the one he had occupied after Charlie died, and ate food without tasting it, silent in the contemplation of the enormous usurpation I was committing. It was late September. The Red Sox (72–90) finished that season ninth in a ten-team league. John had been very annoyed with them, as had I. This was no time for me to be trespassing in his chair. We had matters to discuss, matters we had been working on, without the success we craved, for exactly twenty years.

I know it must have been a weekend morning when they first took me to Fenway Park. John and Charlie had to work on weekdays. We drove to the train station in North Abington in the Studebaker. John was at the wheel because Charlie had rammed his first car into the back of the garage when he brought it home, and never drove again. Two dapple gray horses and a carriage he could handle; automobiles he could not. His son had to drive the car. How much we depend on our sons, and how much we depend on our fathers.

The announcer at Fenway Park that day in 1946, as he does these days, gave first the batting order for the visiting team. Today I cannot tell you with certainty who opposed the Red Sox. I think it was the Philadelphia Athletics, managed still by Connie Mack in his black suit, but I could not

7

take an oath; it probably was the A's because they finished last that year, and Boston won the pennant (104–50), making tickets scarce, and neither my grandfather nor my father had the clout to get good seats for games with contending teams. But that is still surmise: I had to go back through the records to refresh my memory of what must have been the Boston batting order.

Leading off, and playing center field: DiMaggio. DiMaggio, playing center field.

I do not recall for sure who pitched for us that day. It may have been Dave ("Boo") Ferriss, who opined forty years later that the strike zone had changed a great deal since his '46 season (25–6, 3.25 ERA)—he said that nowadays it's between the top and the bottom of the belt buckle—or Tex Hughson (20–11, 2.75, an incredible feat for a Fenway Park pitcher), but some faint, insistent chime of memory says it was Joe Dobson (13–7, 3.24).

Batting second, playing shortstop: Pesky. Pesky, playing shortstop.

The crowd had been quiet in the sunlight while the visiting team's lineup was read, but cheering began with the announcement of Dominic DiMaggio's name. Johnny Pesky got the same respect.

Batting third, and playing left field: Williams. Williams, playing left field.

There was a great eruption. Those who had cheered the names of the leadoff batters turned up the volume a full crank while some of those who had been relatively quiet started to boo.

All of us who live and work in New England, including Johnny Pesky, firmly believe it far superior to all other places on the globe (as, for that matter, does the *Boston Globe*), and we are boastful about the advantages we enjoy, except for the damned weather. Sometimes we exaggerate a bit (and we think we do *that* better than it's done elsewhere,

too; we exaggerate by understatement). Other regions contend that their universities and colleges are as plentiful and as good as ours; we smile forgivingly. Other cities claim that their medical schools and hospitals are at least as good as ours, and we observe mildly that then there must be some other explanation for the regular arrivals at Logan International Airport of ailing Arabian potentates, Greek shipping magnates, South American millionaires, European royalty, and celebrities of international renown in need of expert care. We do not deign to notice suggestions that other states breed politicians equal to ours, regardless of whether the comparison is based upon measurement of acuity or corruption; that statement is beneath derision, and the person making it is merely pitiable. And when they start talking about writers, we don't even listen; ever since before the Revolution we've had more and better practitioners of that eccentric trade than any other part of these United States, and the ones we didn't grow here hurried in as soon as they possibly could.

And we also know, beyond a peradventure of doubt, that in the last four decades we have been privileged to harbor a disproportionate share of the greatest professional athletes playing American sports. Those of us in our middle years can truthfully claim as our own, and have seen with our own eyes: Bob Cousy, Bill Russell, and Larry Bird play basketball; Eddie Shore and Bobby Orr play hockey; Carl Yastrzemski, Wade Boggs, and Bobby Doerr play ball.

But anyone in full possession of his wits and enough facts will concede that the most nearly perfect athletic record of this era was compiled by Ted Williams. Playing left field. For the Boston Red Sox. And that, in keeping with our history, we did not appreciate it.

Playing first base, and batting fourth: York. York, playing first base.

For some reason or other, the Detroit Tigers in the first winter after the war shipped Rudy York (his '45 figures were

.264, 18 homers, 87 RBI's) to Boston in exchange for short-stop Eddie Lake (.279, 11 homers, 51 RBI's). York responded with 17 homers, a .276 average, and 119 RBI's.

Playing second base, and batting fifth: Doerr. Doerr, playing second base.

I do not think I have ever seen a hitter more dangerous with men on base than Bobby Doerr. Charlie told me that, and he was right. Doerr finished that year at .271, with 18 homers, and he drove in 116 runs with a total of 158 hits, 50 fewer than Johnny Pesky's team-leading 208 hits (.335), 18 less than Ted Williams's 176 (.342); 38 of those hits were home runs, but his RBI total was only seven more than Doerr's. He was a superb second baseman, certainly the best I have ever seen in a Boston uniform (although I do admire Marty Barrett). The only justifiable complaint that anyone could utter about his election to the Hall of Fame in 1987 was that it came about thirty years late (he retired in 1952 and became eligible in 1957).

I suppose the announcer with the pebbles in his throat must have proceeded on that day in 1946 to accord George ("Catfish") Metkovich (right field, .246, 4 homers, 25 RBI's), Hal Wagner (catcher, .230, 6 homers, 52 RBI's), Rip Russell (third base, .208, 6 homers, 35 RBI's), and whoever was pitching that day the public respect that they merited, but I do not remember it today, and I did not remember it back on October 11th and 12th of 1975, when I took first my daughter, Susan, and then my son, John, to sit in the bleachers with me and watch the Red Sox split the first two games of the World Series with Cincinnati (6–0, 2–3). Neither did I remember it in the fall of 1978, when I called the attendance lady at Milton Academy and told her that I wanted John and Susan to be dismissed early so I could take them to the play-off game with the Yankees. ("Certainly," she said, "and I'd like to say that you're the first father who's called today and told me the truth.")

What I do remember about that first trip to the ballyard, every time I go there, is that my grandfather and my father solemnly presented a great gift to me that day in 1946, perhaps without being fully aware that it was theirs to give, or how much it would mean to me after they were gone. I go there now, and the announcer speaks of Burks leading off, and playing center field, and while I hear that I can also see myself as a child, sitting between my father and my grandfather in third- or fourth-row seats out beyond the right-field foul pole on a hot summer Sunday back in 1951, when Clyde ("Dutch the Clutch") Vollmer was in the middle of an inexplicable hot streak (he hit 22 homers that year, nearly a third of the 69 he totaled in his ten years in the majors, and drove in 85 runs, more than a quarter of his career 339). I recall how my father became both disgusted—when the Red Sox fell behind early, struggled back within hailing distance of the lead, falling back, once more—and concerned that Charlie, by then nearly eighty, with a history of heart disease, would perish from the sun if not from his frustrated rage. John suggested that we leave. Charlie would have none of it. The game went into extra innings (if my memory is correct) with both teams in double figures, and Charlie raged aloud while my father worried. Then the Red Sox pulled it out (Vollmer did it, I believe), and we collected our belongings and went, exhausted, home. I see more than tonight's ball game when I go to Fenway Park.

The courts of the United Kingdom in the early nineteenth century began to grapple cautiously with a concept new to the law: whether a someone unintentionally damaged in person or property ought to have a legal right to collect monetary compensation from the person who had caused the harm. Farmers sued each other because one, digging a well on his own property, had inadvertently tapped an underground spring that released and flooded a neighbor's holdings. Travelers injured by escaped domestic animals alleged that the

owners had failed to take proper measures to confine them—
at least one, attacked by a wild beast, went so far as to assert
that anyone keeping a bear, or a lion, or leopard, should
have expected that sooner or later it would get loose and
hurt a passing stranger. The purchaser of land thereafter
rendered useless by a shift in the flowage of a tidal river said
that the seller should give his money back.

To each of those protests, the persons whose innocent
actions had caused the woe responded that they hadn't meant
to commit them, and therefore should not have to pay any
money to the victims. Furthermore, they argued, the sufferers had either blundered into the damaging situations, or,
once into them, had failed to keep a proper lookout for their
own safety.

Out of all this controversy emerged what is now known
as the legal specialty of tort law, and a lucrative one it is,
too. Vastly oversimplifying the matter: the general rule in
Anglo-American law is that each person, whether actively
causing harm or passively suffering it, is required to behave
reasonably and prudently in every circumstance. The failure
to do so, if some injury results, means either that the imprudent and unreasonable actor must pay the victim, or the
careless, thoughtless victim cannot collect because his own
recklessness was the chief reason for his damage.

That rough definition of what we know as *negligence*
continues to undergo alteration virtually every day in courts
that operate under Anglo-American Common Law (it might
be kept in mind by Red Sox first basemen, and those who
employ them). It is generally short-handed as "The Reasonable Man Rule," and all such cases balance upon the fulcrum
of what the judge thinks a reasonable and prudent person
would either do, or avoid doing, under the circumstances.
That, of course, requires the judge to consider how alert and
informed such a citizen should be. One compendium of the
attributes of that idealized but ordinary citizen states that

he is expected to be aware of the law of gravity, the rise and the fall of the tides, the habits of the animals, and the progress of the seasons. Charlie and John commenced my instruction in that last aspect that summer day in '46, in Section 17, and just as all the Christmases merge now in my mind into one shining jewel of recollection that I prize anew each winter as the nights come earlier to Boston, so all the ball games, hundreds of them, merge with a few exceptions into a long brilliant skein of incalculable value. I got my Christmases from them, and I got my ball games, too, and when you are an only child, what you share, you keep.

I am writing this on a summer day in New England. The sun is out, and the air is soft, and I have two tickets for tonight's game against the Indians. The Princeton sophomore who took his stuffed Snoopy dog to the '75 World Series thirteen years ago will accompany me, and we will make our way with assurance—after all, we've been there before— through the maze of ramps into the evening at Fenway Park. Sherm Feller, a man of many (less important, to me) talents (his musical compositions include a symphony or two and the early rock hit "Summertime, Summertime") will request our attention to the starting lineups for tonight's game. Two tickets; four of us should be there.

2

In the early summer of 1978, Loretta and I had been together for two years. She was familiar with my habits, and we had both become resigned to the fact that the judge presiding over my litigation (by then four years of painful history; it was just as well that Charlie and John weren't around for that—if they'd been alive, it would've killed them) to secure custody of Susan and John was unlikely in the foreseeable future to issue a divorce decree, enabling us to marry, unless I dropped the contest. That I refused to do. So we said: "The hell with it," and took the honeymoon anyway. We went to Paris, where the flowers in the courtyard of the Plaza Athenée were red and thronged by sparrows, and we ate and drank with friends in the Brasserie Lipp on the Boulevard St. Germain. We gorged ourselves at Chez L'Amis Louis in Montmartre, and we dined in elegance at La-Marée at Une Rue Daru. From there we went to La Reserve on the Riviera at Beaulieu-sur-Mer, and from nearby Nice we flew to Rome.

We stayed at the Eden Hotel and we visited St. Peter's (now there was something John and Charlie would have approved of). The Colosseum was small, weedy, and dilapidated; while operating it had accommodated about as many Romans as Cleveland's Municipal Stadium, which seats eighty thousand, so I'd imagined it to be about the same size, but those Romans must have been awfully cramped; it is not. The field is far too small for baseball, whatever its former merits as a site for watching captives fight to the death, or lions have their lunch. Grass cropped up among the cracks in the masonry, and a bunch of scrawny feral cats prowled around, apparently subsisting on food wasted by tourists. I told Loretta better sham naval battles could be staged in Fenway Park, and she reminded me that we were on vacation. I said at least Fenway Park didn't have stray cats—perhaps combats in today's Colosseum engage cats and Christian mice? And she said no, it has rats, and I said she had it wrong: Boston Garden and the Celtics and the Bruins have the rats—Fenway Park and the Red Sox have pigeons. (Fenway has since acquired rats, thanks to nearby construction—the rest of Boston is about to add to its population of them, too, when the Central Artery's torn down and the rodents under that are evicted.)

In the evening we made a random choice of a trattoria on the Via della Purificazione. It was small, perhaps a dozen tables on the first level, four steps up from the entrance, maybe six or eight more on the second level at the rear. It was dimly lighted by candles stuck into Chianti bottles centered on the red-and-white checked tablecloths—the proprietor was plainly a traditionalist. The ashtrays were black plastic and advertised Cinzano. We ate fine braccioli pizziola and fresh bread, and washed it down with Chianti. The manager inquired in English whether our dinner was satisfactory, and we assured him that it was. I said it was so good I was surprised his place was not more crowded. He looked sad and said only the tourists had been dining out since terrorists had kidnapped Premier Aldo Moro the preceding week. He said Americans especially should understand, after what we had gone through with assassinations. Loretta told him she had worked for RFK's presidential campaign, and he said: "Ah, then you do know."

At the next table there were three men who spoke English—to one another, not to us. They discussed measures available to secure a zoning change that would enable them to convert land set aside for the expansion of a cemetery in Boston's West Roxbury section into highly valuable residential property. Bribery figured prominently in their conversation, not that it was ever named. "He'll do it," the fattest man said. "Of course he'll do it. *After* we do something. They always do it, all of them. They've been doing it for years. All you got to do is know your way around, and that nothin's gonna happen until you do some things, and then you do the fuckin' things, and then the fuckin' thing *happens*. Don't make it complicated—it's a simple fuckin' thing. I'm not saying that it's easy—just simple is all."

The check was small for such an excellent dinner—every check in Italy is small, after a good fling in Paris—and the steep cobbled streets outside were silent in the darkness. Loretta said she could understand why an Italian would be upset at the abduction of his premier. What perplexed her was why Bostonians vacationing in Italy continued to scheme compulsively so far away from home. I said that was the way we were, and travel didn't change us—we just brought it all along.

We went back to that restaurant for lunch the next day. The three men from the next table were not there. We had not finished our meal when the manager tearfully asked us to leave without paying. It was not because we had misbehaved—the gunshot body of Moro had been discovered in the trunk of a car, and he wanted to close up.

We took the train from Rome to Florence and ate melon and prosciutto, and we drank robust wine from the Piedmont. In Florence we dined in the quiet evening lighted with gas lamps at a small restaurant overlooking the Arno and the Ponte Vecchío. We rented a car and drove north toward Innsbruck. There was snow high in the Alps, and it was not a very good car. We played the radio as the car labored up the mountains and then threatened to break loose on the descending slopes, and we listened to Italian introductions of American rock 'n' roll records that had been popular when we were in high school. Then we came to a long tunnel—at the Brenner Pass—that crosses under the border between Italy and Austria. On the other side of the tunnel, the sun was out, but the mountains blocked the radio signal we had been receiving. I fiddled with the dial and found another station. The voice was Ken Coleman's. I had found by chance the American Armed Forces Network, broadcasting the Game of the Week. Coleman said: "There's a long fly ball, deep, *deep* to center field. Lynn's back, 'way back—*he's got it*." And Loretta said: "Oh, *shit*, I don't believe this."

When Fred Lynn played center field—1974 to 1980—for the Boston Red Sox, we entered the ballpark through the gates on Jersey Street—now Yawkey Way, renamed when owner Tom Yawkey died—and passed through the turnstiles cursing softly but contemptuously "Fragile Freddie," endowed by God with all the ability we coveted so much, but too California-laid-back to employ it steadily. Cold nights found him on the bench, complaining of muscle pulls, thus avoiding the sting that a batter feels when he hits a frozen ball. In his subsequent career with the California Angels, his work habits so irritated Buzzy Bavasi that the general manager said if fastballing left-handers started 162 games a year against his team, Fred Lynn would never play a game.

When Dom DiMaggio played center field—1940 to 1953—we went down the ramp from the turnstiles, and we bought our scorecard-lineups for a dime. Day or night, summer or fall (this was before league expansion and 162 games a season—the Red Sox didn't play ball in the winter, then), it was always cool under the stands. There was a pungent aroma I did not identify until much later—it was beer (neither John nor Charlie drank, or served the stuff in his house; one of Charlie's several brothers, for whom he had named my father, was a toper of remarkable accomplishments who managed to hold a teaching job in Lawrence, Massachusetts, until well beyond what's now retirement age, alleviating job pressures with binges at the Parker House, in Boston, from which my father was obliged to rescue him). It's pretty hard to identify that smell now, too, because it comes from light beer, not worth the cost and trouble of passing it through the body.

When I went to Fenway with my grandfather, Charlie, and my father, John, the scorecards were printed in red and blue ink on pulp and stapled centerfolded in the program; you ignored the blurry ads and opened the document so that the Red Sox were on the top page and the opponents were on the bottom. Then you put the scorecard in your pocket and stopped at the refreshment stand for supplies. The hot dogs were fried on chromium rollers, and the rolls were steamed. (I'd stay away from the boiled franks and cold rolls they sell there today—the french fries aren't too bad.)

Fully provisioned, you turned right and walked down through the brick and cement cavern to the ramp that led out to the grandstand at Section 17. The iron rails were red then, and they are red today. You went up the ramp and you came out behind the screen that shelters the people sitting right behind home plate from those wicked foul balls that slice off the tops of the bats and ring against the steel mesh.

There was no electronic scoreboard out behind the center field bleachers back in 1946. There weren't any advertisements painted high on the walls, either, as there are today

(Marlboro, Miller Lite, etc.) because Yawkey (he died in 1974, having been sole owner of the club for forty-four years) wouldn't allow them; you filled out your scorecard-lineup with a Reynolds Rocket ballpoint pen—mine was anodized red aluminum and my father's was gold; Charlie used his black Schaeffer fountain pen—by paying close attention to the public address system. I know Sherm Feller cannot have been the announcer who first commanded my attention in that ballyard back in 1946; it must have been his father, or maybe his grandfather—only heredity could account for the immutability of that gravelly baritone. "Attention, Ladies and Gentlemen. Here are the starting lineups for today's game." I know it could not have been John Kiley who played "The Star-Spangled Banner" on the organ—he didn't start until 1957, when Yawkey heard him at the Boston Garden and added him to the pageant—but in my memory there were no recordings then at Fenway, and there are none today; at Fenway the anthem is played on the organ. I presume that death has long since claimed most of the crowd that taught me the last two words of the song: "Play ball." But nevertheless, when I go there now and see the lineups on the electronic scoreboard out in center field, I along with everybody else still in full command of matters wait until the PA system comes on to fill out my glossy chromecoat scorecard—purchased at ten times the price Charlie paid when I was a child.

It's generally in the evening now when I get to the games. The twilight in Boston benefits in color both from the air pollution and from the offshore breeze so that the sky is rose near the horizon, turning to pale blue about halfway up the sixty stories of the Prudential Center to the east. The announcer speaks—"Attention, Ladies and Gentlemen. Here are the starting lineups for tonight's game"—and the crowd noise diminishes. "In center field, batting leadoff, Ellis Burks. Burks, playing center field." I suppose the uninstructed must be puzzled by the evident redundancy of public recitation of what's publicly displayed. They are the same sort of naïfs who would not understand why unimpeachably veracious witnesses must take the oath in court: Red Sox baseball is a serious matter, and like other serious businesses it requires some ceremony.

Ceremony is what enables a six-year-old boy, hearing the announcer say: "In left field, Williams. Williams playing left field," and: "At second base, Doerr. Doerr, playing second base," and seeing his father and his grandfather writing all the data down, to know that he has been judged worthy of initiation into the company of men. All novitiates first require the mastery of rituals.

There are better things in life than baseball, many of them. It is better to watch your daughter graduate from a fine school into an acceptance at Columbia. It is better than watching baseball to watch your son graduate from a fine school and to matriculate at Princeton. But what we over-look, sometimes, is that baseball is always there. It always has been. In what Jim Lonborg called "the dungeons of the winter," early February, the equipment trucks will pull out of Fenway Park, laden with the stuff that the regulars will need in Winter Haven, with the pitchers and catchers to report in a week. March will be filled with news from the neat little ballpark at Lake Lulu, where a corpulent Ted Williams, at the shag end of his seventh decade, stands at the mesh of the batting cage and torments a Rich Gedman with pastoral observations: "I am anxiously awaiting the outcome of this next swing. I would expect a ground ball, if he holds the bat that way." The batting practice pitcher delivers, and Gedman hits a grounder. "Now I am anxiously awaiting the outcome of this next pitch," Williams says. "I expect another grounder." Gedman swings and fouls it back. "Well," Williams says, "if he'd've hit it clean, it would've been a grounder."

April will come. So will Opening Day. Then it is a brand-new season, one filled with hope and promise. This is the year that the Red Sox win the pennant, as Bemildred (one of the three mice in overalls—the other two were Bothered and Bewitched) used to say in Walt Kelly's "Pogo" comic strip every New Year's morning: "Wake up, wake up, it's a brand-new year. This is the year the Red Sox win the pennant." And when they reproached him/her for foolishly exacerbating their hangovers, he/she replied: "I may be stupid, but I'm loyal."

I have been that for forty-two years. I have been right three times. That is an .071 percentage, sixty points under Dick Radatz's Boston batting average. The springtime in New England is a lot like your first payday. Back then you had 154 games in your pocket; now 162. You can treat your friends and give presents to your family, and the summer will never end. But it always does, and you get down to the coins of a few games left in September; most years, damnit, the regular season ends and the Red Sox have no games left to play, but four other teams, all alien, contend for what's eluded Boston since 1918: victory in the World Series.

All good novices, once ordained, prize not only their mastery, and the rituals, but the masters who graciously teach them. Each time that I was right, the Red Sox lost the Series.

All former novices continue to prize not only their mastery, and the rituals, but the masters who graciously taught them. My father and my grandfather lie beneath the sod of Holy Family Cemetery, in Rockland, Massachusetts. I think of them whenever I get mad about the team. How angry they used to get. What good men they were.

So this is a memoir and a meditation, and a story about baseball, a game I thought I knew quite well until I began talking to the people who were playing in the major leagues when I was still a boy. It does not seem that long ago, not to me and certainly not to them, still agile and rangy in their later years, still as captivated as they were those years ago by the magic of a game. "It's such a *simple* game," Johnny Pesky said, the chaw bulging his right cheek, a bit of the tobacco juice glistening on his lower lip, "and it's so *hard* to play." But it's not difficult to love, and neither were John and Charlie.

It's sort of like going into a warehouse on auction day. On Yawkey Way, where there used to be a few peanut vendors, there is now a plethora of sausage cooks and souvenir merchants, most of them scofflaws of multiple citations alleging that they don't have the proper peddler's licenses (fines alleged outstanding when the Red Sox won the American League East Championship in September 1988 totaled around $40,000). It's a strident oxymoron: a Bostonian souk raucous in the summer evenings with merchandising cries that flatten *a*'s and elide *r*'s, redolent of greasy smoke and the smell of onions and green peppers singeing. Pennants flap in the air, and everyone walks in the street. Nobody sells gasoline on game nights at the stations near the ballpark—they insolently block the pumps with the cars deposited by the last motorists arriving, gouging them illegally with the fine impartiality that they demonstrate toward those who come early to watch batting practice. Every so often some media commentator rises up in a fine fit of indignation at this practice and demands that the privateers suffer a Bostonian equivalent of the Royal Navy's punishment of being flogged through the fleet down to Gravesend.

Nobody ever does the slightest thing in response. But that is all right: all the public and professional varieties of making insouciant small talk—writing newspaper columns, MC-ing talk shows, delivering wisdom on TV—are tough work in Boston in the summertime, and everyone who's anyone is at the beach, listening to the Red Sox, or watching them off the cable. Nobody steals much of anything in Boston in the summer, and that's the usual grist for the mills. If it weren't for the Red Sox and the mini-industry that surrounds and battens off them, there'd be nothing to bitch about in these parts from Memorial Day to Labor Day. Boston with nothing to bitch about all summer would be the East Coast equivalent of Santa Barbara all year-round—warm, foggy, and bland.

"You certainly did," she said. "I was there and I heard you. You called Don Zimmer a dumb son of a bitch. You stood up in Section Seventeen in the fifth inning of that game and you damned near dropped your daughter, and nobody else was yelling, and everybody in the whole world heard you. And you called him a dumb son of a bitch."

"I don't use profanity at the ballpark," he said.

"The hell you don't," she said. "Mike Torrez was pitching and you wanted him out of there, and you stood up and started hollering. You said: 'Zimmer, you dumb son of a bitch, he's bringing the ball up, goddamnit. If I can see it from up here, the hell can't you down there? Get the stupid bastard out of there.' "

"I did not," he said.

"You did," she said. "You kept doing it, too. You said: 'For Christ sake, Zimmer, you fat shit. If I can see it from up here, the hell can't you see it down there? Get that jerk out of there. They're gonna golf one off him.' "

"Well," he said, "I might have said it to you. I didn't get up and yell it."

"Yes you did," she said. "You did it again in the sixth inning, and you did it again in the seventh, and you got even worse in the eighth."

"Well," he said, "and I was right, wasn't I? Didn't Bucky Dent get off his ass and hit that fucking homer?"

"Yes," she said, "and what you said then. . . . And you're the guy that can't understand where the kids picked up that language. You damned near dropped your daughter on the concrete so you could stand up and scream at Zimmer, and your son's sitting on my lap and he heard it too, and you've got the nerve to deny it?"

"I couldn't help that," he said. "I thought I had four tickets wired. Turned out there's only two. We were just lucky the cop let us in."

"I know that," she said. "Just don't tell me you don't swear at the ballpark."

As it is against the law to overload parking lots and pillage those who must park their cars, so also is it against the law to drink on the streets of Boston. That law too is ignored, especially by the college students who return each fall to Boston and believe that mere proximity to the park is a license to drink beer on the street and snarl obscenities at strangers. Then there are the interceptors: you make your way to the entrances through a gauntlet of insolent fourteen-year-old boys, each of whom pretends to believe either that you have "extra tickets" you had been planning to tear up and swallow, or that you have arrived without a ticket and will be agreeable to paying triple its face value in your desperation to see the Red Sox play. It is a good idea to put your wallet in a pocket where you can keep your hand on it and maintain full alert until you are in your seat.

I have observed as much generally genial disorder in some other places: in the marketplace of Marrakech; on Bourbon

Street in New Orleans the week preceding Mardi Gras; on the main drag of Tijuana after dark, when the fleet is in at San Diego up the road and there's a bullfight the next day. I think it is significant that those establishments, like Fenway Park, have been in operation for a long time.

It takes years to develop a decent patina on a bronze sculpture. Very few institutions merit instant trust upon creation. John O'Hara, for example, and John Updike (who is perhaps amused that his most-often cited work, around Boston, at least, is not one of his splendid novels, or his luminous essays, or his memorable short stories, but rather "Hub Fans Bid Kid Adieu," published by *The New Yorker* after Ted Williams's last game in 1960): what made and keeps such gentlemen in the front rank of American writing is not one book, or two, but a proven record of reliability, year after year, neither of them by any means always successful, but each of them in his career manfully stepping up to the plate, taking his regular cuts. One of the reasons that so many writers love the Red Sox is that a team without a World Series triumph since 1918 validates the writer's constant sense of insecurity, and thus proves he is sane.

For seventy years now the Red Sox have failed to get it exactly right. They have always fallen a little bit short: in the Seventh Game of the '46 Series against the Cardinals; stumbling in the '48 play-offs against the Indians; forced to pitch Jim Lonborg on two days' rest against the Cardinals in the '67 Seventh Game; leaving the tying run on third base in the '75 Seventh Game; doing the same thing again in the '78 play-off against the Yankees, when Bucky Dent got off his ass and hit that cheap home run; blowing the Sixth Game in '86 against the Mets and losing the Seventh Game. That's what writers do: no matter what the reviewers say, we know in our hearts it may be close, but no cigar.

Writers too, like ballplayers, know what it's like to have their miscues lovingly detailed in the morning papers by people who couldn't carry their hats. Writers know how hard it is to get it exactly right, even 30 percent of the time—which is what a premier batter accomplishes when he hits .300. Writers, if they are realistic, know how unlikely it is that they will realize their ambitions 60 percent of the time, which is what a team of twenty-four players has to do to win 97 out of 162 regular season games and have a good shot at a Division title (I know, I know: the Red Sox did it with 89 games in '88, but that was a nonvintage year in the East). And there is another psychological resonance between the two occupations, playing baseball and writing: neither is controlled by the clock (no matter what indignant editors may utter about deadlines). If you set out to play baseball, you must complete a set number of innings with one team in the lead before you can go home. If you set out to write a story or a book, you must complete your task before you can go on vacation. Weariness, boredom, a desperate desire to be somewhere else, doing something else: none of those pleas is acceptable. If you were playing ball at Wrigley Field before the lights went up, and a Chicago curfew fell on a tie score, you had to finish that game the next day or the next visit. If you fail to meet your deadline because fatigue has overwhelmed you before you finish the story, you have to get up the next day, snivel some craven explanation to an incredulous editor, and then go back to work.

Such harmonies are what account for the devotion of the scribblers to the game, and especially to the game as it is played in Fenway Park. It is virtually impossible to perform either trade even close to complete perfection.

The ballplayers, of course, can cite physical obstacles to mitigate their shortcomings. Writers can seldom do that. Common sense—by no means always determinative in baseball management decisions, in the years before towered lights and night games came to dominate the sport—dictated that the pitcher's mound should point the hurler west and the

batter east. When the games began in the early afternoon—
as they did until last year in Wrigley Field—the sun was
nearly overhead. Neither batter nor pitcher nor fielders had
any advantage or handicap toward evening, by which time
the game had usually ended.

The lights have changed all that. Notwithstanding their
brilliance, they do not fully compensate for natural daylight.
Today's batters in the majority of games do not get as good
a look at the pitched ball as their predecessors did. Fielders
confront high fly balls that rise out of the lights behind home

plate into darkness, out of which they plummet back into light again. Pitchers, a delicate breed at best, suffer the disadvantage of lower temperatures at night, even during the summer; a man who has worked up a good sweat before sitting out a long inning while his lineup bats around is much likelier to stiffen up at 60 degrees Fahrenheit than he is at 72 (then there is the matter of the absurdly long season, which we will get to later).

It was the Fourth Game of the '86 Series. Forebodings of imminent November dictated carriage of warm outer garments, but God in His whimsy reprieved us from an early chill and made the October night warm. The field-box seats on the third-base line were excellent. The donor was gracious.

"You see out there in right, just before the foul pole [in Section 7]? I was talking to some people today that're sitting out there tonight. The family box seats. Season tickets, every year, ever since the lights went up." That innovation came to Fenway in 1947. "Their grandfather was the guy that installed them—the towers, everything. And Tom Yawkey was really pleased, and he said to the guy: 'Four seats, season tickets, yours forever. Any place in the park that you want, you did such a good job with the lights.'

"Well, the guy wasn't a baseball fan. What he was was an electrical contractor. So he picked the seats out there in right because they had a better view of his lights. I said to one of his kids today, was she going to the game, and she said: 'Oh sure. Out in right field. If he was alive I would kill him.' They're great if you're after a tan." There are seven towers for the lights.

The Red Sox have traditionally demonstrated similar misguided fealty to conventional wisdom, amending it a little to accommodate exigencies, but generally making mistakes. When they moved from the old Huntington Avenue Grounds to the Fenway in 1912, they situated home plate roughly nor'-nor'east, and the pitcher's mound roughly sou'-sou'west. The reason for the amendment was the shape of the plot available for construction.

The playing field at Fenway Park is more or less septi-lateral. For those who have never seen it—or have seen it without really looking at it: beginning at the flagpole in deepest center field, over four hundred feet from home plate, and continuing clockwise, there is an abrupt jog where the home bullpen juts out into right-center field. There is a low wall separating that and the visiting bullpen in right. Those companionable suites within conversational distance of the rowdier fans in the bleachers were constructed when the Red Sox perceived an advantage might be gained for their young left-handed slugger, Ted Williams, by moving right-field home run territory a little closer to home plate. There is a gangway between the bleachers and the reserved grandstand seats in Section 1, deepest right field; separation is preserved by a chain-link fence topped with barbed wire that continues along the gangway wall of the bleachers. The bullpen pitchers sit on cracked green vinyl cushions under corrugated green tin roofs and dig the green paint off the two wooden steps with their spikes.

On the field, the low wall of the bullpen curves into the long straight line leading to home plate. Behind home plate there is another curve leading to the straight line that runs parallel to the third-base foul line to about forty feet behind the bag. There the left-field grandstand intrudes up and out, leaving about three feet of foul territory until it meets The Wall in left, thirty-seven feet high—plus the screen, twenty-three feet more—that leads back to center field.

The foul pole in right is equipped with a screen that extends up the foul side; a ball caroming it is foul. The foul pole in left is equipped with a screen on the fair side: when Carlton Fisk's homer, still on the rise, hit that wire in the Sixth Game, it was therefore over three hundred feet from the place where he hit it, and at least fifty feet above the spot where it had met his bat. The Red Sox insist that The Wall is 315 feet from home plate. Clandestine surveyors have alleged it's closer to 300. All of the field's enclosure is painted flat green.

The listed capacities of the various seating accommodations distribute 1,568 fans among the twenty rooftop ("sky-view") sections high above the first- and third-base lines (renovations in the winter of 1988 added 600 seats up in the air behind home plate). These are the holders of season tickets, or beneficiaries of such owners, and in Boston it is accounted grounds for boastfulness to hold such tickets. The logic of this eludes me. It's a hell of a hike up two and a half flights of stairs to the roof, exposed to the elements all the way, and the plastic screen, fitted with Plexiglas portholes, behind the seats is gapped to diminish wind resistance—thus unavoidably admitting wind-driven rain. The view of home plate from seat 1B in roof box Section 3, on the first-base side, is limited to the batter's boxes and the immediate vicinity of the plate, so that the viewers of privilege cannot see the catcher crowding the screen for pop fouls. A fan seated in Section 4 of the rooftops on the third-base line has a poorer view of the left-field corner than does a humbler spectator seated down below in Section 25 of the grandstand.

"Well, yes," his wife said practically, "so they are out in right field. But at least they can see what Jim Rice is doing in the left-field corner. *We* can't."

"Who the hell," he said, "who the hell would *want* to watch what Jim Rice's doing in the left-field corner? It's like watching an autopsy. *Once*, maybe, you might want to do it, you had a morbid streak. But *every night*? Forget it. I'd rather rub shit on my head." In '88 Rice was finally displaced by Mike Greenwell, who also has some disconcerting habits when it comes to judging and catching fly balls, but, being younger and faster, compensates better for them.

Below the rooftop boxes there are forty-four "luxury" boxes of varying sizes, sheltering up to twenty-eight citizens. One of them, the "Superbox," rents for $1,800 per game, full bar and catered dining extra. Each of them consists of what can be compared only to a comfortable living room, tastefully couched and chaired, with a wet bar, refrigerator, and private toilet. Sliding glass doors provide access to the open-air seats overlooking the action on the field, but for the substantial minority of "fans" attending games in such elegance, the television set in the living room proves the more powerful lure—looking up from the grandstand, you can see them with their drinks in hand, backs to the game, watching what's shown on TV. While the appeal of a private convenience is undeniable, and almost any beverage served to order is preferable to the beer dispensed to the long lines of sufferers at the grandstand refreshment stands, where they require IDs from everyone, no matter how gray-bearded (Loretta returned pleased one evening from a beer run, reporting she'd been carded; I couldn't let well enough alone: "They do that to everybody"), the voluptuary advantages of the setting seem to be incompatible with going to the park to watch a baseball game. It seems fair to surmise that most of the corporate executives who inhabit those boxes have equally plush amenities at home, where the parking is at least as convenient, the beverages and food are adequate, and the television reception equivalent—so why go to the ballpark?

Under the roof where the swells sit are thirty-three sections of grandstand; and in the elements are ten sections of bleachers. The Red Sox in '88 claimed that the park included 13,250 box seats, 12,202 reserved grandstand seats, and 6,563 bleacher seats, bringing the total of seats theoretically available for sale on any given game day to 33,583. "Box seats" is a partial euphemism; some of them are in fact the seats closest to the field. Most of them are the seats in the lower section of the grandstand. "Field boxes" cost $14; "Box

seats" cost $11; "Reserved grandstands" cost $9; and the bleachers are either $5 or $6, depending on whether one purchases in advance. If snobbery is not an operative factor in one's choice of location, the reserved grandstand seats are completely satisfactory for even the most demanding spectator. They afford protection from the rain, denied to the occupants of the field boxes and box seats, and the brick walls of the park block the wind that chafes the necks of those who paid $12 per head to sit in the roof boxes. But do try to avoid such perches as Seat 1, Row 18, Section 18: there's a stanchion square in front of you that would baffle a contortionist seeking to watch the pitcher and the batter at the same time. It's nowhere near as good a vantage point as what might seem to be the worst seat in the house: Seat 1, Row 18, Section 1, the very last seat in the grandstand way out in deep right field, where all the ballpark is in full view, though lots of it is far away.

The identity of the person in charge of scheduling the National Education Association's annual conventions between 1946 and 1956 is unknown to me; whoever it was showed great perspicacity. The Tigers were home when John took us to Detroit; the Indians when we saw Cleveland. The Yankees were home when we went to New York; the Browns when we went to St. Louis. The Reds had a home stand the year the convention was in Cincinnati, and the White Sox were at Comiskey Park the summer we went to Chicago. John was busy at those confabulations, but never too busy to take me to the ball game, except for the year the convention was in New York City. That year John drove Charlie and my grandmother, Annie, and my mother, Doris, and me to Albany. We stayed at the Hotel Wellington, and John went on to Manhattan. We followed him a few days later on the Hudson River Day Line—I think the vessel was the *Hendrick Hudson*, but it could have been the *Peter Stuyvesant*. We debarked at the 123rd Street pier and took a cab to the

Prince George Hotel on East 28th Street, since become a welfare lodging, but then deemed top of the line. The day after we arrived, Charlie took me to F. A. O. Schwarz, and then we went to the ball game at Yankee Stadium.

In the early Seventies a speaking engagement took me to St. Louis—the Cardinals were home at Busch, and of course I went to the game. In 1975 a magazine assignment that later exploded sent me to Municipal Stadium in Oakland for the Red Sox–A's American League play-offs, and then to the Reds' new plant in Riverfront. In 1976 I saw three games in Dodger Stadium in Los Angeles. None of the other ball-yards I have seen compares favorably to Fenway Park.

That is not to say that some of them in various respects are not superior. The sight lines are better at Riverfront and Dodger; it's pretty hard to get a seat in those parks that offers a partially obscured view, but it's very easy at Fenway. In forty-two seasons I have migrated from Section 17 to Section 29, behind third base, and it's impossible, as the lady said, to see from that vantage point what's going on in the left-field corner. But the Reds play on a rug, and while the game requires both bat and ball, it isn't the same game. And while the Dodgers perform on genuine grass, playing the regular game, they do so before a crowd of people who don't quite seem to comprehend what's going on in front of them. A game at Dodger Stadium disorients a person who served his apprenticeship at Fenway: the people arrive around the middle of the third inning and interpret a 0–0 score to mean they haven't missed a thing. They are perfectly at ease leaving at the end of the seventh, with the score still 0–0, so as to avoid the traffic. I don't understand such conduct.

Baseball at Fenway's an audible game. The clanging of the foul balls off the cage-on-wheels behind the plate during batting practice is merely an introduction. The acoustics of the architectural atrocity are—accidentally, I'm sure—magnificent. When Jackie Gutierrez practiced his whistling bird calls while taking infield at short back in 1985, the whole park resounded with his trills and chirps. The pitchers in the center-field bullpen engage in conversations, not always polite, with the people in the bleachers behind them. When Ted Williams played left field, the fans would overhang the wall at the corner and shout pleasantries to him that implied his parents either had not been married or his pedigree was canine; Williams would not answer verbally, but in his next time at bat he would shell the offending section with line foul after vicious line foul, offering a souvenir to any heckler brave enough to face it. Fred "Fireball" Wenz completed three years in the majors (his last with the Phillies) with a lifetime 3–1 record (4.71 ERA). One sparsely attended night in 1969 I heard a fan somewhere behind home plate shout derisively: " 'Fireball'? *Fire*ball? Where the hell'd you get that name?" And from down the first-base line came an immediate response: "He took it at Confirmation."

Life was better before bleacherites and right-field on-lookers obscenely amended the Miller Lite chant—"Less filling," "Tastes great"—to: "Fuck You," "Eat Shit," and back before Reggie Jackson (then of the Angels) became the object of sexual taunts and the Red Sox found it prudent to terminate the sale of beer at the end of the seventh inning, but it's still pretty good, all in all.

And I still say I never got upset enough at Don Zimmer to use profanity when he left Torrez in.

In 1964 the Boston bureau of the Associated Press took up about half the second floor of the Western Union Building at 230 Congress Street in Boston, on the northeast corner of High Street. There were four broad, tall windows on the northerly side of the newsroom, and there was no air-conditioning. The pavement and the adjacent tall buildings soaked up sunlight during the day and radiated the heat back at night. The windows were kept open, and all varieties of New England's summer bugs entered through them—mosquitoes, gypsy moths, flies. We wrote our copy on three-carbon flimsies and used Olympia manual typewriters that moved around on their tables. We—this was all of us: young guys, old guys, middle-aged guys—came to work in sports shirts and drooped unfiltered cigarettes out of our mouths, squinting against the smoke rising straight in the muggy air.

I had been promoted from Springfield correspondent for the AP to the Boston office at the end of May. There I had answered to no one—except when they called and they seldom did. That situation aggravated a certain preexisting lack of humility. I proceeded to Boston in the expectation I would answer to no one there. Some friction resulted.

The New England news editor was James Calogero. He was in charge of assignments. He was also in charge, at least in his mind, of ordering people around. He was in his early forties, full of himself. I was in my early twenties, full of myself. He had managerial prerogatives that I lacked. It was imprudent of me to respond to his allegations that I was "a dumb Mick" by calling him "a stupid Wop." When I did that, he punished me.

Punishment at the AP in Boston in 1964 was a simple matter for the man in charge. The chief sportswriter was Bob Hoobing, later to become press officer for American League President Joe Cronin. His only backup was Charlie MacGillicuddy. Hoobing was active in the officialdom of New England sportswriters' associations. MacGillicuddy was proficient at making himself scarce when undesirable assignments cropped up. Calogero performed retribution by sending his offenders in their place to Fenway Park.

The 1964 Red Sox were just plain awful. Dick Stuart—"Old Stonefingers," "Doctor Strangeglove"—played first, if that is the term. He led the team with 24 errors and won press box appreciation as "The Ancient Mariner—he stoppeth one of three." Stuart and Manager Johnny Pesky got along with each other about as well as I did with Calogero—Stuart called him "Needle-nose." Carl Yastrzemski despised Pesky and batted .289 with 15 homers to prove it. Dalton Jones, too slow to play third base, played second (there's Red Sox logic for you); the Sweet Swinger from the Bayou committed 16 errors and batted .230. The Red Sox lost 90 of 162 that year, and I swear I suffered through at least twenty of them, thanks to Calogero.

It was a spiritually unsettling experience. Because Fenway is the smallest ballpark in the majors—even today, after

much finagling with added sky-view seats, it accommodates far fewer paying guests than actually desire to attend, and this is true even though nearly 2.5 million tickets were sold for the '88 regular season games—and because I had grown up since 1946 attending exciting games crowded by fans, it was disorienting to arrive early, chiefly for the free, good food and cheap drinks served in the press gallery, and then emerge into the twilight of game time to stare over my typewriter and the nearly empty stands below. (In later years, some of my colleagues of the keyboard became so fond of the refreshments that Red Sox management was forced to shut off the television set in the bar once the game began, thus exiling the writers back out to the press box.) Derision was the dominant attitude among those diehards who still paid to get in, and also among those who were paid to attend, and it was appropriate.

True, the imposing (6'6", 230 lbs.) right-handed reliever, Dick Radatz—also known as "The Monster"—saved 29 of Boston's 72 wins, and logged another 16 (against 9 losses) of his own, in 1964. Then 27, in his third year in the majors, he had an arm like a gun, and good control as well. His freshman season (9–6) had yielded a 2.34 ERA, and he set a pattern that prevailed during his best years: fewer hits (95) than innings pitched (124⅔); roughly three times as many strikeouts (144) as walks (40)—and many of those were intentional. (Radatz was strictly a relief pitcher, never starting a game in the majors, often coming in to face a clever, heavy hitter with an open base to park him. "It was a situational thing," Radatz says today.)

But the reason for his opportunity to appear in 62 games in '62, 66 in '63, and 79 in '64 was all too evident: the Red Sox lacked depth of starting pitching. In '64, Bill Monbouquette's ERA was 4.04; he finished the year at 13–14. Earl Wilson was 11–12, with a 4.49 ERA. Radatz in four-plus years with the Red Sox won 49 games and saved 104, for teams that went 76–84, 76–85, 72–90, 62–100, and 72–90. He was instrumental in winning an average of 25.6 games a season for a team that never surpassed a .500 percentage while he was playing for it.

They also lacked dependable offense in 1964. Not one of the regulars batted .300. Besides Radatz, the only real attraction for the fairweather fan that year was the rookie in the outfield, Tony Conigliaro; in 111 games he hit 21 doubles and 24 homers; the offensive futility of his teammates accounted for the fact that he drove in only 52 runs with such slugging. Darkly handsome, 6'3", he seemed to be the cause of the popularity of seats in the outfield among squealing young women whose surpassing interest in the game was believed to be quite recent, and unrelated to baseball.

"We didn't have a good team at all," Radatz said. "We had a number of individual ballplayers who were outstanding. The Conigliaros, Yastrzemski, Frank Malzone. But Chuck Schilling [second base, '61–'65; 541 games, .239] went home for the winter and put on thirty pounds so he could hit The Wall, and it all ended up in his stomach. The catching wasn't good. We had Bob Tillman, who couldn't hit, and Russ Nixon, who could hit but couldn't catch. Eddie Bressoud's a nice guy, but he didn't have the range at short. I had a great set-up man in Jack Lamabe [in '63 and '64, Lamabe won 16 games while losing 20, with a Boston ERA of 4.88], while I got all the ink. But it's tough to save games when you're behind five runs in the seventh inning."

Dominic DiMaggio lays the blame for those bleak years on Lou Boudreau. Boudreau is an interesting case. A man of many baseball talents, he stuck with the Indians at shortstop in 1940 after a couple of "look-see" appearances in '38 and '39. He was twenty-two years old. Two years later, he became manager as well, and after Cleveland's team jelled in '47 (80–74, .519), logged three very creditable seasons (97–58, .626 in '48, when he outsmarted the Red Sox; 89–65, .578 in '49; 92–62, .597 in '50). He made an indelible mark in 1948 on Red Sox fans and Boston front-office types as well, apparently, when his selection of Gene Bearden (19–7) to pitch the play-off game proved better (Cleveland 8–3) than the one Joe McCarthy made for the Red Sox—Denny Galehouse (8–7). McCarthy resigned in June of 1950, leaving the club in the hands of Steve O'Neill; his 92 games in charge resulted in 60 victories and 32 defeats, a .674 percentage. But in 1951, with Boudreau coming over in midseason, purportedly only to play short, O'Neill's first full season yielded

87 wins against 67 losses, .565, and the Red Sox finished third, with Ted Williams en route the following April to Korea and another stint flying fighters.

Boudreau came in the next year with an ostentatiously public Five-Year Plan. Dominic DiMaggio spends his eighth decade of summers in a house that overlooks one of the prettiest harbors in Massachusetts, and he does not conceal his anger. "That was just great," he said. "Wonderful tenure plan—'I'm going to be here five years.' He wrecked the ball club. Got rid of all his veteran players, disrupted the inner workings of the major club, and then disrupted the minors as well. The damage that he did [in three short years: 76–78, .494 in '52; 84–69, .549 in '53; 69–85, .448 in '54] lasted over thirteen years, until Dick Williams came in in Sixty-seven and won a pennant with a club that wasn't supposed to." Whatever magic Boudreau had had in Cleveland was gone; he managed Kansas City to three dismal finishes between '55 and '57 and closed out his career with the '60 Cubs team that finished 54–83, .394, leaving Boudreau with a career record of 1,162 wins and 1,224 losses, .487.

"Cripes," Pesky said, "that first year he had the job, he had four three-hundred hitters sitting on the bench: Dominic, Dropo, Vern Stephens, and myself."

DiMaggio, believing he had at least two years beyond '52, quit three games into '53. Bobby Doerr had retired the previous year. Walt Dropo, 1950 Rookie of the Year with 144 RBI's (tied by shortstop Vern Stephens) and 34 home runs, was traded to Detroit with Johnny Pesky. "It was hard for me, when I was traded," Pesky said. "The years I had in Boston, well, I think if you're Red Sox, well, it's something you're born with, an affection that you have." And this from a man born and raised in Portland, Oregon. "We had a great bunch of guys. We could pick up a club. And then they were all gone." The long decline had begun.

Still, though they suffered much pain, a sizeable remnant

of The Faithful did persist. My father was one of them. He ambushed me one summer morning after I'd passed a hideous night for the AP at the ballpark and proposed that I spend my day off going to the game with him. I hurt his feelings by displaying my reluctance. "John," I said, "they're terrible. They're awful. And this is a day game after a night game. They'll all be hungover and play worse'n last night." He looked reproachful. "The Browns weren't good, either," he said. "I took you to see them." We went to Fenway that day—I knew when I was whipped.

We also had a good time, even though the Red Sox stunk out the joint again. My father and I adhered strictly to the rule that members of different generations refrain from discussing anything of genuine emotional importance—carrying it, as is the invariable Irish practice, to an extreme. (After the war, when steel was again available for the manufacture of such frivolities as motorcars, John and I had the first man-to-man discussion I can recall occurring between us. At issue was the sobering question of whether he would remain loyal to Norfolk Motors, the Weymouth dealership that had sold him his DeSotos, or shift his patronage to Carl S. Burrell Oldsmobile in Rockland. In favor of Norfolk was his pleasant association with them and the existence of a herring run behind their garage where we could go and watch the alewives swim up from the ocean to spawn. Tipping the balance in favor of Burrell was his shared membership on the board of directors of the Rockland Cooperative Bank, started by Charlie and several fellow Micks to offer home financing to struggling lower-middle-class Irish shut out of loans at the Protestant banks. The '47 Olds 98 two-door was light green on the hood, roof, and trunk, and dark green on the fenders, and it should have been lemon yellow.) Religion dominated our shared lives—if Holy Family parish sponsored a triduum (three nights of haranguing by a Capuchin friar), or a mission (seven nights of haranguing by the friar—the one I remember

46

is Father Celsus, who was actually a pretty nice guy once you got him away from the pulpit), we not only vied for the misery each evening, but further mortified the flesh by attending daily Mass before the sun was fairly up. And it did not end there, either, because if St. Bridget's in Abington sponsored a triduum or mission, we faithfully attended that, because St. Bridget's was one of the seven churches that we visited for prayers on Holy Thursdays. At such events we were assured that the phosphorescent fires of Hell awaited all whose hormonal urges got the better of them, where they could expect to find themselves in rooms adjoining those who drank or saw *Forever Amber*. Perforce that same Jansenistic creed circumscribed our conversations in those lives we shared; we never afterward discussed the forbidden conduct, abiding in the view that to do so would sully both the speaker and the listener.

I do not by this recitation mean to suggest that I grew up in a layman's replica of a silent monastery inhabited by Cistercians of the Strict Observance. When Annie was still around, we could muster at most only five people for a Sunday dinner, but the talk was endless. We talked about politics and books and the daily clutter of ordinary small events that occupy most of our lives, maligned our enemies, lampooned absent friends, made fun of one another, and talked about baseball. Charlie, John, and I talked about baseball because it was pristine, free of the emotional freight that more personal subjects portaged. The Red Sox were among the codes that we used to reassure one another that indeed we realized we shared life and appreciated the company.

For that kind of fan—the one who really needs the game—even a badly played contest can be enjoyable, as long as he's not obliged to write about it. (Every critic I have ever met—book, drama, movie, restaurant, art, or dance— shares the same experience: the development and application of the expertise you need for the job takes all the fun out of watching the event, because you have to keep some critical distance in order to report.) The seductiveness of baseball is that almost everyone with an abiding interest in it knows exactly how it should be played. And secretly believes that he could do it, if only God had seen fit to make him just a little bit less clumsy.

In that respect baseball is different from basketball and football. Any fool can see that one must be unusually tall or unusually large to participate in those affrays. (There have always been a number of massive baseball players, of course—Ted Williams stands 6′3″—but large size is not required. Until recently most of the players were of approximately average stature; only pitchers and first basemen seem to gain a noticeable advantage from above-average height.) It is different from hockey, too—skating by itself is an art separate from stick handling and slap shooting (as is assault and battery while wearing those skates). Baseball is a game played by generally normal-size men whose proportions approximate those of the majority of the onlookers, and whose feats are therefore plausibly imagined by the spectator as his own acts and deeds. Radatz, somewhat outsized for a baseball player of that era, did not set out to play it. "Heck, I wasn't a baseball player—I was a pitcher. And besides, I didn't even think I was a pitcher. I thought I was going to be John Havlicek when I went to Michigan State. And then one day Fordie Anderson, the coach, was scrimmaging us, and this black kid was shooting hoops on one of the other courts. And he missed almost every shot, but then he'd grab the rebound and just *stuff* it. Well, the stuff was a big thing in those days, and the coach said: 'You guys just keep on with what you're doing, and I'll be right back.' That kid was Johnny Green, played fourteen years in the NBA, and put my stuff on the pine, and I said to myself: 'Well, I guess it's baseball. Or nothing.' "

That afternoon in '64, when we saw that bad ball game,

48

my father was fifty-eight and weighed close to three hundred pounds; he knew he was too old and too fat to play, but he also knew he had played in his youth, and that he knew enough about the game to have coached the Hardwick High School team to a rewarding season over thirty years before. Frank Malzone that day may not have realized he was in the tenth season of a twelve-year career (destined to end after eighty-two games in an Angels uniform), but John did. He studied Malzone at third for a few innings, his forearms resting on his knees, and then he sat back and folded his arms across his stomach and said flatly: "He's all done."

"At least he's still trying," I said. "That's more'n lots of them can say."

John shrugged. "He's proud. That's fine. But time doesn't care about pride. It should, but it doesn't, and he's getting too slow."

That is why Douglass Wallop's novel, *The Year the Yankees Lost the Pennant*, was so successful, in print, on stage, and on film (as *Damn Yankees*): because the people who buy books and theater tickets include a fair number of middle-age men who know that pride doesn't count, but believe nonetheless that it should. They too would cheerfully sell their souls to the Devil ("Applegate"—Ray Walston played him in the movie; never has there been a better, slyer, more insidious Devil, and that includes all the productions of *Faust* that I have never seen) in exchange for one brief season of heroical baseball matching Joe Hardy's consummate season for the Washington Senators.

That appeal is intensified for those whose interest in the game evolved at Fenway Park. The children who bring their gloves to their seats in hopes of a perfect foul ball are not being silly, really; lots of foul balls carry through the short territory outside the baselines and end up in spectators' hands. Because the people sit so close to the field, they can see with greater acuity what the players are doing to disguise—and compensate for—weaknesses, and they can also see whether it works. It is not mandatory to study such behavior in order to enjoy the games, but it does magnify the pleasure, and after a while it becomes a habit—"a while" being those years between eight and twelve when one's father or grandfather nudges you and tells you to observe that the shortstop's habitually playing back on the fringe of the outfield; either he's grown too slow to short-tackle grounders to his left or right (Vern Stephens) and needs that extra bounce, or he's got a cannon for an arm (Rick Burleson) and can throw runners out from deep in the hole. A confident left-fielder in Fenway depends on The Wall to rebound line drives sharply back to him, and therefore plays shallow, giving away the possible double that will result anyway if the batter rams a line drive low into the corner. (Carl Yastrzemski kept his skills sharp by playing his position during batting practice and by having batting coach Walt Hriniak hit fungoes off The Wall before batting practice had even started. Yaz played baseball with the same devotion to practice that Larry Bird brings to basketball: both too slow for their sports, they honed their abilities by virtual total dedication to improving the skills that God had given.)

Because of The Wall, it is fatal for a pitcher to bring the ball up to right-handed pull hitters—or to inside-out left-handed swingers such as Bernie Carbo. When you see that happening you know that pretty soon there is going to be at least a two-bagger, high off The Wall, or a genuine Fenway home run.

The canard, probably established by Ring Lardner, is that all baseball players are stupid. Maybe they were in Ring's day, which was sixty years ago. A good many of the ones I interviewed, nearly thirty years ago, were tangle-tongued and rude, and few of them had read two books all the way through. Radatz: "I was probably one of a handful of college graduates playing in the big leagues in nineteen-sixty-two. I don't think there were more than twenty-five or thirty in the big leagues then."

But there is a difference between ignorance and stupidity. It takes fierce concentration, along with unusual ability, to become one of the 624 players rostered today by major league clubs. The young men who achieve such eminence devote most of their energies to it. If at twenty-four they are deficient in their knowledge of philosophy, and their grammar is defective, well, few of us could hit the curve. About ten years after Conigliaro and I had a nasty exchange in a postgame interview, he invited me to attend the opening of his par-three North Shore golf course. I asked him if he was sure he had the right Higgins, since I no longer played that game those days, and hadn't when I had. My tone was cool. "Look," he said, "I know, I know. But I was awful young then. You older guys, you college guys, you all picked on me." He had a point—I'd been twenty-four that summer.

My friend Gerry O'Neill played baseball in college. By itself this meant he was at least one step above me in what John McPhee has called "the levels of the game." Since Gerry batted over .400 playing first base in college, and I had all I could do to bat .280 in high school, the likelier approximation would be that he was three or four levels above me.

Baseball is the cruelest sport. Almost every other occupation permits the mediocre performer to seek out his plane of maximum competence, however low, and then lumber along it until he reaches retirement age. Baseball ruthlessly eliminates every single young recruit who that year lacks the talent to join that .0000024 percent of the total population of the United States that plays major league baseball (we will leave Latin America and Canada out of this calculation; to include them would only serve to make the statistics more depressing).

Emboldened by his record in his senior year in college, Gerry suited up and went to one of the major league scouting camps, where middle-aged men with steely eyes study the volunteer prospects and pit them against one another. "I knew I was finished," Gerry said. "I got up there and I couldn't even see the ball, let alone hit it. I took my cuts and I tipped my hat, because that pitcher really was good. I felt bad when I went away from there, because I knew that for me it was over. But I also knew I'd gone up against a guy who was a cinch for the majors. And when he got there I would brag that I'd batted against him once, and I knew he'd make it easy.

"He got released in Single A. Didn't have the control."

5

Those of us who started following the Red Sox forty years ago, and more, tend to compare today's stalwarts unflatteringly to those we saw back then. We forget a number of things.

The "America" encompassed then by the American League was that corner of the republic between latitude 44 degrees and 36 degrees, and longitude 68 degrees and 92 degrees. The team traveled by train no farther west—or south—than St. Louis, and no farther north than Detroit. The "Nation" frequented by National Leaguers was similarly restricted to the same northeastern quadrant of the country. Eight teams in each league met one another twenty-two times a year, refining their knowledge of one another's capabilities in ways impossible today, when "America" includes Toronto to the northeast, Seattle to the northwest, Anaheim to the southwest and Dallas–Fort Worth to the south. And if the dozen teams in the "Nation" now bounded by Montreal on the north, Atlanta to the southeast, Houston to the south, and San Diego to the southwest have an easier scheduling time of it than the unbalanced seven-team Divisions that play in "America," they nevertheless confront similar problems getting acquainted.

Radatz disagrees with me, and he should know. "There's liaison scouts now—Sam Mele, Frank Malzone. You're going in to play KC, and you're playing in Minneapolis, the time you get to KC, *before* you get there, Malzone's back with reports *this thick*." He holds his right thumb and forefinger apart to indicate two inches. "There's no problem about knowledge about who you're playing."

There is a difference, though, as Radatz said, between pitching and playing ball. Pitchers, whether on road trips or at home, face exactly the same task: somehow throwing the ball into the strike zone without permitting the batter to hit it. The strike zone is sixty feet, six inches away from the rubber on the mound, regardless of whether that mound and the plate are laid out in New England or in the Pacific Northwest. And the batters that they face when they play the Royals in Kansas City are likely to be the same batters they opposed in Fenway, complete with the same strengths and weaknesses the pitchers sought to avoid and to exploit back at home there in Back Bay. True, the pitchers must take into account the varying dimensions of the parks and adjust their deliveries accordingly when calling upon hosts with shallow power alleys. But few pitchers endeavor to throw fly balls anyway, especially to right-handed batters in Fenway—what they want are grounders. (That is why Roger Craig's split-finger fastball and its variant, the cut fastball, have become so popular: the reduction of rotation on the ball makes the ground ball more probable than the fly ball when the batter makes contact with it.) And then there is the frequency factor: a given starter must contend with a park uncommonly inhospitable to him—as Oakland's Memorial Stadium, for example, seems to be for Roger Clemens—only once during each visit. But the batters have to stare at that four-hundred-foot-deep center field sixteen or eighteen times each in four games. A hardscrabble team that fabricates runs out of ground singles, hit batsmen, walks, steals, and enemy errors may be little inconvenienced by playing in a foreign arena big enough to serve as a landing field for Boeing 747s, but the Red Sox, at least in my memory, have never fielded such a team. They have depended on doubles and homers, and those can be hard to come by in a commodious facility.

Dom DiMaggio agrees with me. DiMaggio was not a pitcher. DiMaggio in his career hit .323 at home, .273 on the road. His slugging percentage was .464 at home, .374 on the road. That was not an anomalous record. Through 1983, Wade Boggs averaged 53 batting-average points higher at home than on the road. Joe Cronin was 51 points better in Fenway than when he was traveling. Bobby Doerr: 54. Fred Lynn (in Red Sox uniform): 80. Jim Rice in his first ten years hit 43 points higher at home than out of town, and Yaz was plus 42. Even Ted Williams, that student prince of hitting, relished home cooking: he averaged 33 points more in Fenway than he did in alien quarters.

"It was everything," DiMaggio said. "The backgrounds had a lot to do with it. The fans in the triangle"—Section 34 and Section 35 of the bleachers, in center field—"used to wear white shirts at Fenway, and you couldn't see the ball. Finally they started shutting off that area, so it was just green. And you could see the ball better." They've opened it up again since DiMaggio retired; now there are two platforms for TV cameras at the apex of Section 34, but for most home games the rest of that section and Section 35 are occupied by customers.

"Then there was the wind," he said. "You knew the wind in your own park. When I saw that wind, the flag blowing in, over The Wall, I went to the opposite field. A player who wasn't there all the time wouldn't know that. Wouldn't know

the ball'd just hang up there if he hit it into that wind. It took me a long time, in places like Comiskey, to figure out the wind. It really swirls in there. I remember coming in on a fly ball, and I didn't misjudge it, and that thing just took off like a fan-tailed pigeon sailing in my face. Well, Fenway's just as tricky if you're not familiar with it. The Wall keeps beckoning, and you really need someone on your ball club that knows what it's like."

On the average, every American League team each year plays 11.5 regular season games against each of thirteen opponents. True, it's hard in the abstract to play half of a game, although the poorer editions of each team have at times striven manfully to prove the abstraction wrong. (Late in June of '87, my nephew Ted and I conferred at the end of the first that Baltimore, playing badly and down 4–0, had no prospect whatsoever of getting to Jeff Sellers, who'd no-hitted them, 1-2-3, at the top of the inning. "It's over," he said, and I agreed. In the top of the second, Sellers was gone, having retired not a single batter and having allowed six long drives. Three hours later the Sox had won, 13–9, the hitters for once contriving to make up for their pitchers' profligacy with early leads.)

Williams and Lonborg separately agreed on the importance of early offense as a defensive tool. "I didn't agree with Earl Weaver about much," Williams said, "but on one thing he was right: 'Get one run? Get two. Get two? Get three. Get three? Get four.' Especially in a place like Fenway, where so many things can happen. Get as many runs as you can."

"It makes a lot of difference when your team scores runs," Lonborg said. "If they score runs early in the game, that takes a lot of pressure off you, in the sense that you don't have to be nearly so fine. As you do with your pitches when no runs're scored. You know: guys run on you. And there's another thing: you never know, when you warm up, the stuff you have in the bullpen, whether you'll have it for the game. Whether it's really going to be the stuff that you have when you get on the mound. By that I mean there are many instances when a pitcher'll warm up in the bullpen, and have absolutely magnificent stuff, his best fastball, his best curveball, and then never get through the first inning."

American League officials, nothing if not ingenious, have complicated that fact of human limitations. Each year until the 1987 season, they borrowed one of the eight Eastern Division clubs to play two more games against each Western team than did any of their competitors. For 1987, they "balanced" the Divisions by moving the Twins from East to West. So now each team in the West plays twelve games against each other team in the West, and ten games against six of the seven teams from in the East, twelve against the seventh. Clear? Of course it's clear: two Divisions of seven teams each are as mathematically impractical as one of eight and one of six.

Rotation of the assignment means that in a given season Toronto, New York, and Boston could find themselves in a dead heat in September, with two of the competitors obliged to exhaust their pitching staffs against each other and the third browsing among the generally weaker teams of the Western Division, saving its strength while picking up wins. It also means that a team mounting a late charge, as Milwaukee did at the end of '88, is helpless to affect directly the outcome in its own Division—Milwaukee finished up playing in the West, with only the lorn hope that the Red Sox, the Tigers, and Yanks, lurching around miserably from Fenway to Tiger Stadium to Yankee Stadium, would damage one another enough to let the Brewers finish first. They didn't, the Red Sox managing to lose ten of their last eleven while winning the Division (and also providing a chilling preview, that proved all too accurate, of their destiny against Oakland in the play-offs—swept in four).

No matter which club is another club's strongest rival, at most they will confront each other head-to-head twelve times a season, ten fewer than under the old eight-team arrangement; at worst, they will meet but eleven. The National League system isn't perfect by any means, but at least inter-Division play is the same every year for every team in each Division, although at most seven fewer times each season than the old structure provided. Because baseball is a game of guile and animal craft, a civilized form of espionage, reduction of exposure to a team's strongest enemies has inexorably improved the survival prospects of players less fit, while diminishing the alertness of the best. They probably think that it's nice to relax, but the paying customers don't like it and suspect it leads to bad habits not easily shaken when the iron comes to town.

Then there is the matter of surroundings. It used to be that every game was played on natural grass, under the open sky, and most of them were played in daylight. The dimensions of the parks varied, as they do not, increasingly, today, but the basic field conditions did not—Fenway was always considered a premier playing surface; Comiskey Park was not. While it is still possible—and therefore customary—to groom real grass according to management's assessment of the home team's strengths and weaknesses, only those teams that play at home on grass can exercise the option. (Fast teams with good bunters keep the infield grass long, to slow the grounders down, and the outfield grass shorter, to speed up those getting through the infield—Fenway's impeccable infield is mowed vertically and horizontally, and short, so that nubbed infield hits will get to Sox infielders faster than fleet opponents can make it to first base. The outfield is mowed in concentric semicircles and also coiffed for ball speed.) Radatz: "The first time I walked out on the turf [at the Houston Astrodome, when he was pitching for the Expos] I said: 'Can I spit on this?'" He could, and he did, and so did many others: in 1988 the Astros parted with $23,000 for a carpet-cleaning machine warranted to remove juice stains (the Astros' farm team in the Florida State League, apropos of absolutely nothing, is called the Osceola Astros—for the county—instead of the Kissimmee Astros [for the community where they play], and if you say that last name aloud, you will know why).

Teams whose home turf is manufactured by the hand of man now groom the team to the turf, seeking out batters whose ground-pounding swings would horrify a traditionalist like my father. "Keep your swing level," he would repeat, hopelessly, as I topped the ball again. But a talented fleet-footed lad who can manage to make contact can hit major league pitching today, whacking the ball hard into the ground and beating the infielder's throw off the sky-high bounce. Turf in effect permitted the invention of a new abomination: the infield high-hopper became a base hit.

"It's definitely changed the game," Williams said. "I still teach the same way, when I run my hitting schools. I tell these high school and college coaches, 'Teach the kid to swing so that the bat travels in the plane of the ball, with a little uppercut at the end.' But there's no question that the turf has changed the game. I tell them: 'I still think this is the way to hit. But if you've got a kid who's scared at the plate, and can really run, teach him to chop down a little and then run like hell for first.' " He looked like a man who had just been advised to have dental surgery.

Jim Lonborg pitched seven years in the National League (Phillies, '73–'79, 75–60), where turf is far more prevalent (the Red Sox meet only four teams on turf during the regular season: Kansas City, Texas, Seattle, and Minnesota). "The hitters [on the rugs] used a chop as opposed to an uppercut swing. It's a game that depends on speed. Not that many teams have that much speed, that obviously dominates. St. Louis is the obvious example."

Radatz: "It's altogether different on the rug. The ground ball? The infield hopper? It's a base hit, and it's not right. I said this twenty years ago: 'We can put a man on the moon, and we can't grow grass under a dome?' I'm sure they could. I think it's changed the game."

"No question that it has," Williams said. "I was talking to Johnny Bench, couple years before he retired, and I said to him: 'John, you don't seem to be comfortable out there catching anymore.' And he said: 'No, not with the turf. Now every runner's got a fast track. If it rains, well the drainage is much better, and they get off the dirt around the bag and they're gone. You'd need a thirty-oh-six to gun them down. I don't have a chance any more.' "

And there are many who believe the turf significantly increased the probability of disabling leg injuries. Running on cement, even when it's padded with polyester bristles, is not good for the muscles and bones. "I would think so," Pesky said. "I know it hurts some guys. I think it would have more effect on outfielders than infielders, just because they run farther."

So, when we compare the record of Ted Williams to that of Carl Yastrzemski or Jim Rice, without adjusting their statistics for such changes in playing conditions, we seem at first impression to do an injustice. But since justice would require the application of complex formulae that most of us are too slothful to master (baseball, after all, is a sport we spectators cherish precisely because it is not work, but an escape from it), we find superficial justification in our argument of fairness because those two eight-team leagues, after all, played but eight fewer games in the regular season than do today's twenty-six. It seems as though what Williams could do in a 154–game season is a fit measure for what Rice can do in 162.

Oddly enough, when we poach the results of such scholars of the sport as John Thorn and Pete Palmer—their book,

The Hidden Game of Baseball, is just what the subtitle says it is: *A Revolutionary Approach to Baseball and Its Statistics*, intelligible even for the lazy fan who can't keep a checkbook straight—we find that our gut instinct was right. Applying their computerized standards, they determine that Ted Williams in nineteen seasons was worth about 97 wins to the Red Sox—victories that would have been losses but for his contributions at the plate *and in the field*. (It was fashionable to sneer at Williams as a fielder when I was a kid because he was unpopular in the press and because he had studied The Wall the way Einstein studied relativity. He seldom had to hurry much to field almost any carom—so he was charged with jaking it, lollygagging around and dreaming while awaiting his next turn at bat. That was a bad rap.) That is an average of about 5 wins per season, in major league history second only to the 5.3 seasonal average compiled by Babe Ruth in his 22 years on the field.

All this really just tells us that Ruth was a giant, which we already knew, and Williams was second-best—which most of us suspected (Ty Cobb was worth an average of about 3.8 wins a season; Mickey Mantle, 3.9). Carl Yastrzemski's 23 years, using the Thorn-Palmer Method, garnered the team 47 extra wins, a little over two per year. In his first ten seasons, Jim Rice's contribution totaled 22.6, most of them before he developed fully his present nasty habits of overswinging into double plays, striking out with two on and two out, and initially charging fly balls hit over his head. It isn't realistic to ask why a player's not a Ruth; it is fair to ask whether he is making full use of his abilities, and to inquire further whether management has staffed its club with capable performers.

The factors that Thorn and Palmer, Bill Elias and Bill James, and the other venerables of the Society of American Baseball Research (SABR) manfully use to calculate realistic comparisons only partially include how the country has changed externally around the game, even while the game was going through its own convulsions. Carl Yastrzemski's last season included roughly 35,000 miles of air travel, five or six times what Williams underwent on trains in his most productive years. Carl Yastrzemski's stomach by season's end, he said, was so confused he wasn't sure when to eat; Yaz had to pass through all four time zones several times a year; Williams struggled with but two, and at a pace much less demanding upon the circadian rhythms of sleeping and eating.

The older veterans, required to perform in only two different time zones, tended to discount the effects of commuting among four. "Travel never bothered me," DiMaggio said. "We played all those day games then. We might start a western trip by flying to St. Louis, but then when we were finished there, we'd get on a train, travel three hours, and be in Chicago." And travel fatigue? "Never gave it a thought." Bobby Doerr's recollection is similar: "I don't know—when you're younger, maybe it doesn't affect you as much. We traveled between the cities on trains, and you always had your bunk-type thing back there you could go back to. Relax a little bit. It never bothered me." Pesky and Williams stressed the compensatory advantages of contemporary accommodations and facilities. Pesky: "They always go to a good hotel, and they always go to a good restaurant where they'll get food that'll help 'em. When he [Yaz] got hungry, he'd eat just about anything that was in the clubhouse." That last observation may have been a bit of slyness on Pesky's part: Yaz was careful with his dollars, once rescuing from Dwight Evans a leather jacket Evans was preparing to discard, and wearing it for another two years; interviewers who smoked carried a spare pack of Marlboros for conferences with Yaz.

But both Williams and Pesky on further reflection conceded the probability that jet lag takes its toll: "I just don't know how much," Williams said. "I used to get on a train on Sunday and travel to Chicago, but I didn't play till Tuesday. I don't think it affected me, but maybe it did. But I was twenty-four, twenty-five, then. I'm sixty-five now." He was in fact sixty-nine. "What do I know about these kids, what it does to them?" Pesky: "It takes you at least two, three days to adjust when you go from east to west. And you're playing all night games. Got to have some effect. To me it's a wonder there aren't more players now that've got stomach problems."

Lonborg: "Look, it's at least better than basketball, or hockey. At least you go into a town, and you stay there two or three games. Those guys, I pity them. It has to affect their play, one game and then the next city, for another one." Lonborg was indisputably correct: statistics compiled during the 1987–88 season of the National Basketball Association showed that the home team won 78 percent of the time.

Dick Radatz was more certain: "The time difference does affect play. And it's tough. Bobby and Dominic were very clean-living men. As opposed to a myriad of other people. There were a lot of hard-drinking, hard-living people. You never did get to bed. You're always playing cards, and drinking—the whole bit. It was tough."

Then there is the development of the fan. The Dwight Evans we started watching play right field in 1972 worked through 1988 (leaving out the first-base excursions) when at home on the same patch of real estate that Al Zarilla roamed from 1949 to 1952, but Zarilla played a different sport before a different kind of critic. Perhaps because we fancy ourselves so much more sophisticated about the business than we were forty years ago—and because media so regularly and unctuously assure us those who come to Fenway are baseball's mandarins—we employ a double standard when we evaluate Evans's play. We want him to be better than Zarilla, and he is, but we also want him to play the same game that we remember, and he can't. Maybe Zarilla didn't, either.

When we were growing up, the only games we saw were the ones that we attended. John and Charlie were avid patrons, but they also had to work, had lawns to mow and obligations. In those days when doubleheaders were scheduled for most Sundays, we saw perhaps an average of a dozen games a year, about four more than I manage to attend in my adult years. But John and Charlie and I, to see those dozen games, went to Fenway Park no more than seven or eight times, about the same number of visits that I manage now each season (except 1981, when I boycotted the place after management the previous December cynically contrived Carlton Fisk's departure).

"I really miss those doubleheaders," DiMaggio said. "You'd go back in the clubhouse. Some of the guys'd shower, and the others just towel off. Have a sandwich and a soft drink. 'We got you the first game? Okay, we're gonna get you again. You got us the first game? Watch what we do, the second.' It was nice. I really miss those doubleheaders. But of course they can't play them anymore. They need the money from the separate admissions."

Well, they could. They could play separate admission doubleheaders in the warm days of summer and obviate the need to play night games in the cold days of springtime and the freezing days of autumn—if Boston had bested Oakland in the '88 American League Championship Series, Game Three of the World Series would have been played at Fenway instead of Oakland; the temperature at game time in Boston that night was low in the forties, and by the time the game would have ended, it had dropped below 30 degrees. Unseasonable? Sure. Unusual? Not really: seasonal temperatures are averages of several daily temperatures for a given period, and in the northeast quadrant, those daily temperatures vary wildly. Baseball in cold weather is like skiing in late May: it can be done, but it's not much fun to watch, and it doesn't look like the real thing.

But this is what Dick Radatz said, characteristically iconoclastic: "There's one thing that's better now, about the game—there's no more scheduled doubleheaders. Those damned things were killers."

The real thing is the only thing that will satisfy today's Boston fan. The reason that today's Red Sox follower is more demanding, more knowledgeable—and less forgiving, too—sits in his living room, and there's probably another one in the kitchen and a spare in the bedroom, as well. While the experience of watching the game on television at home is an exercise in sensory deprivation compared to attendance at the park, it nevertheless enables the housebound to watch many more games per season. As the spectators have become more sophisticated by watching television when they can't get to the ballpark, so television has become more sophisticated in the visual coverage that it offers—more cameras in different vantage points; slow-motion replays; freeze action. That new scoreboard behind center field in Fenway now delivers reruns of the plays just made and inspires as well repetitions of the crowd reaction as they study it again on the screen. If I were an umpire, I would hate that thing. But all of that televised convenience costs money to produce, and those mundane considerations have prompted many changes in scheduling, such as replacing those Sunday doubleheaders with a surfeit of night games. The drawback, from the fans' viewpoint, is that the brand of baseball played now is probably inferior to what was played before. The advantage: those weary after work have more opportunities to monitor the sport with their own eyes.

If I go to eight games a season, that probably represents somewhere between 5 and 10 percent of the games I actually see in part if not in whole. (My grandfather used to bang the chair arm and shout when the Sox were playing badly; I can hit the channel zapper and avoid the passive frustration—although I seldom do that. I've seen so many causes, hopeless in the fourth, turn into double-digit free-for-alls that the Red Sox often won, that I can't bear to turn away.)

The difference between listening to the game on the radio and watching it on television is as great as the difference between watching it on TV and going to the park. I do not believe the radio announcers of the Forties and Fifties were any gentler on the shortcomings of the local heroes than are the Ned Martins and the Bob Montgomerys in the TV booths today—indeed, it's hard to imagine how they possibly could've been. (I must say, though, that Sean McDonough in the first year of his tenure as a TV announcer in 1988 proved forthright indeed, to the point at which he made his sidekick, Bob Montgomery, more incisive as well.) But when a Ned Martin or a Jerry Remy fails to comment harshly on misjudgment of a fly ball I have seen with my own eyes, when the camera in the sky-view box above the first-base line shows me Jim Rice in the corner, bungling the play, I can form a better judgment of the actual quality of play than radio allows. Curt Gowdy in the Fifties and Sixties did not, to my recollection, comment adversely on the radio very often when a Boston player showed up out of shape; neither does Ken Coleman today. Those announcers, after all, travel with the team, and if only from a sense of politesse are inclined toward charity. But the cameras are merciless, and the viewers are better served. And Martin made a good point, too, in the green easiness of Winter Haven, where he'd come to practice with his new partner, Remy, the former Red Sox second baseman (the Red Sox having thus acquired the cognac of broadcasting teams—Remy Martin): the cameras exonerate the announcers from some of the obligation to offer judgments.

Then there is the manner in which television has gradually elevated the standards we apply to the locals. Network and satellite broadcasts of games far away have remedied to a considerable degree the lacunae in my education caused by John and Charlie's indifference to the doings of the Boston Braves and the rest of the National League—an indifference so widely shared in the Boston of my youth that Lou Perini uprooted the team and took it off to Milwaukee (the Braves had just brought up a kid named Aaron—Henry? Could've been). The technology permits me to sit peacefully on my couch and watch the Yankees play the Tigers in Detroit, of a Saturday afternoon. That enables me to compare players I have never observed in the flesh to players I see at Fenway Park. It enables Bobby Doerr to watch American League games in his home on the Rogue River in Oregon and make judgments he could not have made thirty years ago.

The Thorn-Palmer Method credits Yankee outfielder Dave Winfield with producing in his first eleven years three more victories (25.2) than Jim Rice delivered in ten, and this while Winfield was being platooned by managers in thrall to George Steinbrenner. Watching Winfield on national TV, I can form the opinion—quite possibly wrong—that an athlete of that calibre, discontented in pinstripes, might be an improvement over a lackadaisical one at home in Fenway. (One of baseball's charms for the freight-bearing layman is the permission it grants to develop and defend possibly erroneous views, but this one was shared by the Red Sox front office: back a few years ago, they thought they had a done deal, Rice for Winfield, but Steinbrenner changed his mind. History repeats itself: Ted Williams told Don Gillis of WCVB-TV, Boston, that the owners of the Red Sox and the Yankees one night during his career had a liquid dinner in Manhattan at which they agreed to swap Fenway-perfect Joe DiMaggio for Stadium-tailored Williams. The next morning, Williams said, "One of them, I don't know which one, called the other one and said, 'I don't think we'd better do this. One of us'll get lynched.' " Then he paused. "But I never wanted to play anywhere else besides Fenway.")

The players who understandably complain that today's ticket holders are fiercely—often, profanely—unapprecia-tive of their efforts must in their turn understand that many of those aficionados have observed those replays, reverse camera angles, and slow-motion pictures of competitors whose performances their own eyes have told them are su-perior.

Paradoxically, that same technology, while elevating the sophistication of the fans, has significantly helped diminish the number of superior players available today. Radatz: "The minor leagues have been ruined by television. The simple analogy is this: Here's a guy sitting in Decatur, Iowa, or wherever, making eighteen, twenty grand a year, with three kids, and they've got a minor league team there that happens to be in third or fourth place. And it's going to cost him three or four dollars per head, and you've got to go to McDonald's before—that's another twenty-five-dollar tab. He's gonna have a few beers at the ballpark, and the kids're gonna want a souvenir, so it's a seventy-five-dollar net—which he can't afford. So he says: 'I'm gonna watch Detroit and Boston on my TV tomorrow, and drink my own beer, and it's not gonna cost me nothin'.' "

Because the minor leagues cannot compete live on the

performance level of the major league players on television, the clubs and the leagues go broke. Radatz: "When I came up in Sixty-two, I think there were fifty-six minor leagues— not clubs; *leagues*. When I got out, in Seventy, there were nineteen. Most of your independent owners today are marketing men, not baseball men. You go out to the park and the big event's not the ballgame—that's just something that just happens to be going on the same night. The big thing's that they're giving a Cadillac away. Or that somebody can win a trip to Vegas. Ballgame doesn't matter at all."

The dramatic contraction of the minors means that the traditional methods of development and selection of the fittest prospects no longer work. Radatz: "I don't believe that the average baseball player reaches his full potential before he's about twenty-four, twenty-five. Somebody like Tony Conigliaro: he is your exception." But now there's a shortage of places to train the average player, to cultivate what potential he does possess, to show patience with late-bloomers. "I saw Rico Petrocelli at one of our Old Timers' games, and I said: 'Jesus, Rico, I'm seeing guys out there that couldn't've played Double A ball when you and I were playing.' And he said: 'It's a fact. Guys're now learning how to play baseball up in the big leagues.' And sometimes they're not even learning there. I think it's quite obvious. Why is it that so many pitchers now don't know how to field their position? Because they don't care anymore—not just the players—management, too. When I was in spring training, they used to hit us ground balls. Day after day: bang, bang, bang. So you'd know how to make the play, you got in those situations. But they don't do that anymore. It's a lost art—like bunting."

Pesky does not entirely agree. (This is perhaps because his position as special assistant to General Manager Lou Gorman intensifies the attitude common among members of select fraternities: virtually all the veterans that I interviewed manifested determined reluctance to criticize adversely the performances of their predecessors and successors. Lou Boudreau was the only person excepted from that courtesy. I took it as a tacit, tactful, but firm declaration that someone who has never undergone the actual tribulation of endeavoring to play the simple game that is so hard, before thousands of jeering onlookers, could possibly appreciate the pain that attends failure to succeed at it. They willingly specified their own shortcomings, and regretted them, but they politely resisted invitations to comment on the deficiencies of others. Pesky, overheard comparing one player's efforts in the field to those of "a monkey trying to fuck a football," implored omission of the awkward fellow's name. That was a reasonable request.) "Sometimes you do have to learn to play, when you're in the big leagues. We get the kids coming up now, and what we look for are these things: hit, run, throw, and catch a ball. The basic skills. If the kid has that, then we can teach him when to do what. It's so much different now than it was when we started to play. There are so many other things. We played ball all the time."

Williams put it more succinctly: "There're more diversions now. When I grew up, my house was about as far from the field as that shack [an equipment shed about 150 yards to the east of Yawkey Field at the Winter Haven complex] is from that field. We'd be on the field in the morning. Then go home for lunch, and come back to the field in the afternoon. After dinner, well, we even had lights. It was all we did. Now you've got boats, and motors, and vacations, and tennis—all those other sports. In my day, kids didn't have so much. So we played all the time." He told Gillis, in interviews conducted for the WCVB-TV program "Ted Williams—Splintered Thoughts," that he gave up tennis in his youth after breaking two gut strings ("Didn't have nylon then") in his racquet at a tournament, and his mother, contemplating the thirty-cent cost of their replacement, told him, " 'You'd better find a cheaper sport.' Well, I had a bat."

We all had bats in those days, even those who had no business with them. I did not meet Peter Blewett and his mother until they moved to Rockland early in the Fifties. They had lived through the Blitz in London, emigrating to America for a better life some few years after the war. I must have been eleven or twelve; Pete was a year or two older when they took the second-floor apartment in the house fronting on Reed Street, diagonally across two backyards from the house on Pacific Street where I lived with Doris and John. Pete taught me how to play chess, an occupation for which I was as naturally qualified as for baseball, and he commenced my education in classical music—an education that remains disorganized and unsystematic to this day, but that is not his fault. For revenge I taught him baseball. We did not play catch—why I do not know, but throwing a baseball back and forth in Rockland was known as "having a pass." In the summers, family vacations and stints at summer camps serially removed Bob Dunn from the list of available players (Bob was a pretty fair country catcher, and he could hit well, too), Bobby Fobes (about on the same level as Pete and I were, but either more realistic or more easily discouraged), Bob Bedard (probably the best player among us, but inclined to hang out with an older crowd and seldom on the duty roster), Jack Metivier (good arm, not bad at the plate, but gone to camp most of the summer), but for some reason or another Pete and I always seem to have been around. When we tired of throwing and catching the ball in the street, we went over to my house, where a tall brick chimney, which served both the living room fireplace and the oil burner in the basement, presented an admirable backboard for simulation of high fly balls, and the concrete risers of the front steps, if artfully employed, returned hot grounders and high hoppers indefatigably. Both practices were as sternly forbidden by my father as the pepper games outlawed by signs on the fences of most major league parks, but my

father augmented a teacher's salary in the summer first by
driving an ice cream truck for Hendrie's and later by teaching
summer school, so it was pretty easy to get away with it. In
the spring, before the frost was completely out of the ground,
we played baseball at Memorial Park, various four-man and
five-man versions of it, anyway, and in the autumn we resisted the demands of our friends that we put away our gloves
and bats in order to play touch football. In the winter we
played basketball in the high school gym, and longed for
springtime, even for the mud that covered us when the thaw
was finally complete and the sod was soft and slick, and in
time each year it did come, and we could play baseball again.

I did not think of the implications when Pete and his
mother flinched each summer at the prospect of the Fourth
of July fireworks displays at Memorial Park (they especially

disliked the aerial bombs); I guess I assumed that being British they were sheepish about having lost the Revolution. I did not ponder at all what a strange and remarkable thing it was for an English boy and an American boy to base a close and delightful friendship upon chess, Beethoven, and baseball. It seemed like the most natural thing in the world, and now that I have thought about it from the vantage point of years, I think that was what it was: the most natural thing in the world. I do not see how anyone who liked the first two pastimes could fail to love the third. And so though we were light years away from Williams and Pesky in baseball ability, at least in one respect we were very much like them—we spent our days playing ball. So did most of the other boys, then, just as the old Red Sox said, and some of them in time became the big leaguers that we watched, before the summers changed.

Exacerbating the shortage of dependably trained players is the expansion of the leagues. (And if regular rumors are to be believed, it isn't over yet—Denver really wants a team, as do several other cities too small before television to support a franchise, but now prospectively robust markets. Floridians incensed that the major league teams visit them to get in shape, then take the polished product north for serious competition, have real cause to hope; it seems unlikely that the leagues will neglect much longer the fourth-most-populous state, already a proven market for the sport, even though a threatened White Sox move down there last year was scuttled when Chicago agreed to spring for a new stadium.)

It used to be that sixteen teams hired 400 players at relatively modest wages to contend for championships. Now twenty-six teams retain 624 at most munificent rates. While it is true that the population has dramatically increased, and the occupation is now open to racial groups excluded until 1947, superior performers remain as scarce as ever, and average Joes are not as good. (It is possible, even for Ted Williams, to exaggerate this phenomenon: "Expansion should've improved the hitting, because there aren't as many good pitchers to go around. And it did, the first time. But not the last time. I know one thing: there're people around today with just as much ability as I had, but the averages aren't there." The appropriate response seemed to be incredulous laughter; after a moment, Williams joined in.) While it is likely true that the relative proportion of truly outstanding athletes to clumsy oafs like me is probably pretty much unchanged, the increased demand for their services has dispersed them among more games and more teams, so that the fan of a given sport sees fewer outstanding players in a given season than in days gone by.

Outstanding, in baseball parlance, is after all a relative term: it means that the player *during his generation* regularly exceeded the levels of performance achieved by his competitors. A careful inspection of statistics yields some surprises, at least where Red Sox players are concerned. Bob Stanley, for example: much maligned as he has been, and hampered greatly by overall staff deficiencies requiring him to shift from long relief to spot-starting, and back to long relief, hindered as well by injuries, he entered the '88 season with 104 career wins, 91 losses, 123 saves, and a 3.60 ERA. Those are Hall of Fame statistics, but you'd never know it from the catcalls greeting his appearances at Fenway. And consider Frank Sullivan: from '53 through '60 he spent eight years pitching for declining Red Sox teams (and delighting reporters—when the team's charter flight returned to Logan Airport after a disastrous road trip, he cautioned his mates to scatter at the bottom of the steps, "so they can't get us all with one volley"). He won 90 and lost 80, with a 3.47 ERA; he was ten games above .500 during years when the entire team managed to win 622 against 607. Thorn and Palmer calculate that his '55 season (18–13, 2.91) accounted for five wins that the team would not have gained with an ordinary pitcher in his place, and constituted the 99th best season of 100 recorded by any major league pitcher in this century. Sullivan was outstanding that year, as Stanley has been since he joined the club in 1974.

Runners competing since Roger Bannister broke the barrier of the four-minute mile (May 6, 1954), then a stupendous achievement, now routinely turn in times 10-percent better. There is a theory, so widely advocated as to intimidate challenge, that competition over decades in any given sport tends toward parity of performance: if there are relatively few .300 hitters today, it's because the pitchers are better. If there are relatively few 20-game winners around now, it's because the .260 hitters are now good enough to box their ears for them.

Baseball, while drawing upon a population pool roughly 50 percent greater than it was in 1950, faces hiring competition nonexistent then. Danny Ainge, running up and down the parquet of Boston Garden in his Celtics underwear, first ascertained in a Toronto Blue Jays uniform that his skills as a major-league infielder were unlikely to bring him the acclaim and treasure that he had in mind. When Bobby Doerr coached the new Jays, his pupils included Jay Schroeder, since promoted to, and demoted from, the starting quarterback position with the Washington Redskins (and later traded to the Raiders). Bo Jackson was forthright when he completed his football career at Auburn in 1985 and declared his election to play baseball (for the Kansas City Royals) instead of pro football: he said the probability of an injury prematurely ending his career in baseball was so much less than in football that he figured to make more money taking strikes than crackback blocks. (Then, in the midst of the '87 season, he mused he might play some football for the LA Raiders in the baseball off-season, "as a hobby." Royals management did not conceal their dismay at Jackson's invocation of his contract clause, permitting such adventures, but the

Raiders, in a rare rebuilding phase, waited patiently to receive him. He performed superbly in pads, as he did again when he returned to the Raiders after the '88 season with the Royals, but the first year he did it John Madden appraised it as a long-term bad idea. Drawing upon his experience as coach of more than one hundred Raider victories and a Super Bowl championship, the NFL TV commentator predicted in '87 that Jackson would play, at most, one more season of professional baseball: "What happens is that when you play in the National Football League, you get beaten down to where you can't lift your arm the same way. Bo might dodge a bullet his first year, but I'm sure he won't have full range of motion in his shoulder after a couple years in the NFL. He won't be able to play baseball.")

Such options did not exist when Jackie Jensen opted for the Yankees after a sterling football career at USC (he came up in 1950). While he could have played pro football, the pay was nowhere near as good and the profit motive easily resolved the issue. Eighties prospects face no such choices: the disparity between the potential rewards of, say, pro basketball and those of pro baseball are minuscule for players at every level (what counts now, or should, is comparative length of average career—baseball is about three times longer).

Stellar athletes of the Eighties first surface when they're young, are speedily identified by networked mentors in their sports, and often emerge as phenomena before they're old enough to vote. Unbelievers are invited to contemplate the professional tennis circuit, where each season seems to feature a new teenager beating the bejabbers out of some old fogey who isn't thirty yet. Bobby Orr was a teenager when he electrified first the Boston Bruins and then all New England soon after. Most talented kids are specialists before they finish Little League baseball, use up their eligibility for Pop

Warner football, or make the starting fives of their high school basketball teams in their freshman years.

Back when Ted Williams was a downy cheeked youth, short of cash to get his racquet restrung, baseball was about the only professional sport offering such chances. Williams was twenty when he played his first major league season. Tony Conigliaro hit twenty-four home runs for the Red Sox in 1964 and celebrated his twentieth birthday the following January. When today's kid with the reflexes of a cobra, the eyesight of a fighter pilot, and the strength and speed of a sprinter comes along and shows an affinity for sport, long before we ever hear the name that kid has been channeled in the direction that crafty adults deem most likely to make him—and sometimes, them—rich and famous. If the kid at twelve has the build of a shortstop but the range of a first baseman, hits short line drives with lots of topspin—and lives to hit them—the chances are that some tennis pro will take him aside and give him some friendly advice: vicious short line drives are money in the bank in tennis, but not much use even in American Legion ball (and if he's good enough, the manufacturers of racquets will supply his needs, for free). The question today is not whether such an athlete can modify his play and acquire new skills adequate to give him a chance in professional baseball—it is whether his natural abilities are better suited to a different calling, where the potential rewards are at least as great, and fewer compromises will be necessary.

Williams disagrees with me ("Modern players are just as motivated—they just don't play as much.") but I think mobility among all sports has led to a lack of motivation among players of all sports. Pesky is on Williams's side: "Sometimes they give you an attitude like they don't care. But they do." I don't think so. There is a consistency of inconsistency in individual performances over the extended season, even allowing for the cataclysmic effects of even minor influences upon finely tuned performers. Wade Boggs stands out not only because he annually bats at least .350 (he could stand some improvement in the RBI department, though), but because he performs every game as a .350 hitter should. Therefore he is given standing ovations. Bob Stanley annoys Boston fans because he is perfectly capable of throwing nine innings of shutout ball one night, to win 1–0, and because he is also perfectly capable of losing his concentration in the fifth inning of his next outing, with the score at 0–0, and leaving the mound with his team down 4–0, bases loaded. He is also capable of getting too fat, and that is his own fault. We do not like it. Nobody in his right mind is claiming that Stanley should be blindingly effective every night (although each of us does demand exactly that on the nights we happen to attend), but almost everyone thinks he should be reliable; since he isn't, he gets razzed. Stanley does not like that. It's hard to blame him.

It could be that by this behavior we defeat the accomplishment of our own wishes: our loud complaints may account for the curious fact that Rice-on-the-road has compiled dramatically better offensive statistics than has Rice-in-the-Fenway, remarkable when one considers what that proximate Wall ought to mean to a right-handed slugger batting half his season against it. Like Williams, he doesn't appreciate jeers; especially from his "friends." Unlike Williams, he doesn't take sufficient pride in his work to perform at his best despite the abuse, or to lay off the groceries and keep himself in shape.

Bobby Doerr cannot recall being hammered by the Boston media or being insulted by the fans. Reasonable enough, because he was perceived as a workman who always gave his very best. But those who won't, or don't, get ridiculed pitilessly. That is why the obloquy continues, ever mounting in volume. Much of it issues from the throats of men who did not grow up hanging on broadcasts of tennis matches, Celtics games, Patriots games, or Bruins. We did not have, as prospective loyalists, the menu of options that both players and viewers now enjoy. (Well, Jack Metivier did dote on the Cleveland Browns and insisted that Otto Graham was the best athlete who ever lived—the rest of us thought he was odd in that respect.)

Secretly, both Charlie and John believed that if only God had shown the good sense to endow them with keener vision, faster hands (Bobby Doerr has the front paws of a polar bear), quicker feet, and better luck, they not only would have played for the Red Sox, but would have gotten the clutch hit, struck out the crucial batter, or made the leaping catch that would have won the Series. Naturally, I imbibed that belief, and so did all my friends. In the summer mornings, when enough of us were home, we got up and ate cold cereal and took our bats and gloves to Memorial Park and shagged flies for one another until lunchtime. We called it: "hitting some out." After lunch we took our bats and gloves and went back to Memorial Park and shagged for one another till supper. In the evening, after we ate, we took our bats and gloves to Memorial Park, and took infield practice until the bats flew out of the pine grove into the gloom, and we could not see the ball anymore. We were short on ability, but we did believe.

She was a woman of mature years who liked to read five or six books a week and had found a way to make a living at it. The perpetrator of such a coup acquires a certain habitual insouciance that leads in time to the expectation of similar resourcefulness from others facing long odds. Anger and frustration set in when the expectation is not rewarded. That is what happened to Maggie Manning, the *Boston Globe*'s book editor, in 1975.

That year the home-away situation appeared to favor the American League champion Red Sox, who embarked on four of seven in familiar surroundings with a regular season .580 percentage (47–34) at Fenway and a for-Boston-astonishing .608 (48–31) road record. But the '75 National League champion Cincinnati Reds were even more of a statistical anomaly: compiling a .605 (49–32) record at home, they had recorded a remarkable .654 (53–28) out of town. Plainly this was no year for those of sporting blood to bet the ranch on the home team, either way, regardless of the usual edge.

Boston had taken Game 1, 6–0, at home on October 11th, Luis Tiant five-hitting the Cincinnati Reds. My daughter was seven then, and inclined to believe that Red Sox baseball was a social outing, even when the best I could do was two seats in the bleachers. (Sad to relate, she persisted in that frivolous misapprehension, and in '86 quite shamelessly joined her friends at Columbia in celebrating the Mets' World Series victory—I disinherited her, of course, and had the locks changed on the house.) She was complacently happy that the Red Sox had won the pennant, but by no means experienced the first stirrings of mingled hope and stubborn fear that gnaw at the true Red Sox follower when things get off to a good start.

The Big Red Machine was not disabled, and came back at Fenway on the 12th, 3–2, as reliever Rawley Eastwick made the Reds' two-out, two-run rally stand up. At Riverfront two days later, the Sox, down 5–1 after five innings, got one back in the sixth on Bernie Carbo's homer and two more in the top of the ninth on a homer by Dwight Evans.

That game was one of the toughest I have ever watched. For one thing, the press office had seated me next to Roy Blount, Jr. I do not know quite how to characterize Blount's occupation. The usual sobriquet is "humorist," but it's too tame for him; he's more of a cynic gone antic, with occasional intervals of utter battiness, and it's very difficult to devote full attention to anything else while sitting next to him. He introduced his lovely companion as the reigning Possum Queen of Georgia, airily declaring that as one of the contest judges, he had been instrumental in her selection. He confided that she had then assisted him in choosing the most beautiful possum among the animals shown at the second part of the pageant. He did not seem to be troubled by the inference that his vote might have been impaired by lust— indeed, he specified that lust had been his sole motive. He went on to describe in detail the superiority of the Georgia

Possum Pageant to all other beauty competitions. He grounded this opinion in the candor of its rules, which openly admit that the judges intend to eat at least one of the two winners. Blount's voice has solid timbre, and it carries well. He does not like to hurtle to the end of things, especially when he finds himself surrounded by an appreciative audience. The fact that he knows at most three or four of his perhaps fifty or sixty listeners hinders him not at all; indeed, it seems to impel him to shift from narrative to aria, his almost caloric Southern accent coagulating like a big warm muddy river choked with catfish in the sun, eddying and swirling, seeming never to progress but always and inexorably moving on. It must have taken him close to the end of the regulation nine innings to complete his monologue.

That comic relief was an errand of mercy for the Red Sox partisan that night. It is certainly the only time I have ever decamped from an important Red Sox loss weak from laughter. In the bottom of the tenth, Cincinnati's Cesar Geronimo singled, and Ed Armbrister bunted him to third and himself to second—not an easy thing to do, and accomplished only because Armbrister thwarted Carlton Fisk's effort to field the ball, causing Fisk to throw wildly into center field. A mighty protest issued from the Red Sox, but no interference call was made. Joe Morgan singled Geronimo home to take the game, 6–5. The next night Luis Tiant made five runs in the third stand up for a 5–4 win, but Cincinnati was undaunted, and on the 16th made good use of two homers by Tony Perez (who played 1980–82 for the Red Sox) to win, 6–2.

That sent the road show back to Fenway for the Sixth Game, October 21–22. Boston got three in the first; Cincinnati got three in the fifth, two more in the seventh, and one in the eighth. As a chilly midnight approached with Cincinnati leading 6–3, Maggie stood up and expressed her disgust.

"I'll see you people at home," she said, and stomped down the stairs toward the runway.

In the bottom of the eighth, with two runners on, Bernie Carbo unloaded a prodigious shot over the fence in left center, bringing loud cries of rapture from the stands. In the bottom of the ninth, the Red Sox loaded the bases with none out, but then succumbed to an attack of the chronic ailment that has plagued them ever since I can remember: LOB. Perhaps all teams leave men on base in similar numbers, causing similar frustration. Perhaps the Red Sox leave more men on base—eight, ten, twelve per game are not uncommon figures—because they have so many slow-footed hitters who can't score from second on a long fly ball to deep right center; because they wait for the long ball; because they get the vapors; because. . . . Oh, who the hell knows why it is? Whatever the explanation, decades of Red Sox players should be grateful that LOB is not a statistic routinely included in the agate box scores, where the numbers usually record only sins of commission and silently pardon omissions.

The tenth inning passed, Dick Drago in relief of Rogelio Moret (Tiant had tired in the eighth) holding back the Reds, Pat Darcy with the Red Sox in stymie. The eleventh came and went without offensive event, though defense was a different matter—Dwight Evans leaping to steal a homer from Joe Morgan. (What a wonderful ballplayer Dwight Evans has been, sturdy, determined, and steady. It has been a privilege to watch him play these sixteen years and more.) The top of the twelfth was quiet. It was downright cold by then, and damp, in the park, as it often is after midnight in October in New England. No Roy Blount was in sight. A thin fog swirled around the steaming lights. We huddled in our parkas, hands jammed into our pockets, and when Cincinnati took the field for the bottom of the twelfth there was a note of desperation in the hortatory cheering.

Darcy took his warm-up pitches. Carlton Fisk, going through his fussy rituals—tapping his spikes with his bat, adjusting his helmet, shrugging and tugging at his uniform shirt—stepped up and whacked Darcy's first pitch high and deep to left. The initial shouts of joy subsided into preliminary sighing: the ball was hooking farther and farther left toward the foul pole. Fisk took perhaps three tentative steps down the first base line and began using body English, waving the damned thing fair. It seemed as though that smash flew five minutes toward the yellow pole—and then banged off, fair, into the net above The Wall. And Fisk began to jump, as did the rest of us, who would be unable to speak above a whisper the next day, having left our voices there that night at Fenway Park. Fisk jumped all the way around the bases (ABC TV minions foolishly erased the tape).

We walked back to Maggie's, down Commonwealth Avenue, in the early morning, and we were not cold anymore. We went up to her place, and we took off our jackets, and drinks were offered, and food. And all the time we were there, she looked at us and glared. Finally she said: "You knew this was going to happen, and you let me leave anyway. I hate you all."

The second life of the Boston Lazarus was brief, expiring the next night. Manager Darrell Johnson in the ninth relieved Jim Willoughby, replacing him with Jim Burton, who promptly gave up the winning run on a bloop single by Joe Morgan. Cincinnati, 4–3.

And Fenway really is a graveyard, the last resting place of Johnny Orlando. Orlando was the equipment manager for the Red Sox during Ted Williams's tenure. Though in his playing days Williams was disdainful of writers, fans, and nearly everyone else on the earth except Tom Yawkey, he had a streak of compassionate generosity that he privately indulged. As aloof as he could be toward some of his teammates—who were also aloof from one another; the capsule description of some star-studded teams has been: "twenty-five players, twenty-five cabs"—he showed a lot of kindness toward the people who served them. He gave expensive cars and other gifts to Orlando. When Williams retired, in 1960, Orlando lost his protector, and was shortly thereafter discharged.

Orlando was a drinking man. In that considerable capacity he became friendly with Jack Hurley, a bartender, and that friendship is the explanation for the failure of local papers to record the final resting place of John Orlando, who died October 14, 1974. In Orlando's case, interment was not only private, but in violation of Massachusetts's law prohibiting disposition of human remains on grounds not designated "cemeteries." Hurley, learning of his friend's death, called his widow to make the usual inquiry of whether there was anything he could do.

She didn't think so. The only desire her husband had expressed regarding such morbid matters was that he be buried at Fenway Park. And she knew that was impossible. Hurley disagreed.

Orlando's remains were cremated and put into a vase. Hurley accepted the vase and added a bottle of Heineken beer. He got into Fenway Park in the dead of night (he was partway up the security fence when a truck arrived, so he followed it through the gate). He distributed some of Orlando's remains around the infield and deposited what was left into the sod of left field. Orlando's spirit must have beamed that night a year or so later, when Carlton Fisk circled the bases. And wept next night, when Morgan singled.

It is so damned *hard*, being a Red Sox follower—almost as hard as the game. Three cabbies, off the day shift, sat at the bar in the Cask saloon, on the corner of Brookline Avenue and Lansdowne Street, in the late afternoon. Their names were John and John, and Don. They were in their early fifties. Each of them wore a hat—the first John was wiry and wore a white scally cap. The second John was paunchy and wore a crushed fedora. Don wore a blue cap with a Red Sox logo; he was seriously overweight. They drank draft beers conscientiously, six apiece in forty minutes, and they discussed substantial matters.

"You goin' the fuckin' game or not?"

"Nah," Don said, "I got my class."

"Don't fuckin' go, the fuckin' class. I got a fuckin' ticket. Hurst is going tonight."

"Bullshit 'don't fuckin' go,'" Don said. "I hadda pay, cost me twenny-five bucks, get it changed from days to nights, and that's more'n I make, a fuckin' day. I got to go my class."

"Well, you could fuckin' skip one, couldn't you?"

"I could," Don said, "but if I fuckin' skip one, I got to have a reason. And the ball game's not a reason."

"Think up a reason."

"I can't 'think up' a reason," Don said. "If I was any good at that, I wouldn't be inna fuckin' class. No, I better not just skip a class. I rather go the ball game, but I gotta get my fuckin' license back, 'fore they find out I'm fuckin' drivin' all around without no fuckin' license." He belched. "I'll tell you something, you guys," he said, "shouldn't drink and drive. You prolly won't a hit a thing, but if they catch you doin' it, they'll grab your license from you and then make you go to class. And that class really sucks."

"How you get the fuckin' class, you haven't got your license?"

"Very simple," Don said. "I drive the fuckin' cab home and I get in my wife's car. And she drives me to the fuckin' class, and picks me up afterwards. And she chews my ass out going, and my ass out coming back."

"You drive the fuckin' cab around all day, you haven't got a license," John II said, "so skip the fuckin' class tonight and go the fuckin' game."

"Look," Don said, "I drive the fuckin' cab around because I got to make a living and the cab is how I make it. I *don't* drive the fuckin' cab around because I haven't got no license, all right? I hadda choice, I'd have the license. Only I don't got one, so I have go the fuckin' class and get the fuckin' license back. Before they find out what I'm doing."

"You're goin' to the ball game, though."

"Of course I'm going to the ball game," Don said. "I always go the ball game. I'll think up a reason. But she won't believe me, though." He coughed. "And then I'll be in big trouble, in at least two places, and it'll be a lousy game."

It's hard to care about the Red Sox, not that those who do have any choice. The reason it's so hard is in large part management's resolute refusal to heed the lessons of reality. Baseball is the only game I know of in which the team on defense gets the ball; in every other major sport, the offense gets the ball. This means that each batter is on the short end of 9–1 odds of success, with only the very best having a realistic chance of personally overcoming those odds (by hitting safely) 35 percent of the time. If the pitcher delivers the ball in the strike zone, and does not forfeit his team's advantage by hitting the batter, or issuing a base on balls, the odds are well over two-to-one that the defensive manpower in the field will prevent the batter from reaching base. Consider this the next time you read that the winning team "pounded out" twelve hits on its way to a victory: in a nine-inning game, that means the losing pitcher(s) faced a minimum of thirty-nine batters (or thirty-six, if the home team led at the bottom of the eighth), twenty-seven (or twenty-four) of whom did not reach one base, let alone all four.

Fenway, for all of its structurally exaggerated hospitality to hitters, does not repeal the baseball odds that generally favor defense over offense—it alters them, sure, but it does not annul them. And the team of any given year must play half its games away from Fenway, inhospitably surrounded.

It would seem to follow logically that the people assembling Red Sox teams, like the people rostering competing teams, would seek to bolster defense, perhaps sacrificing some offensive ability to run up football scores in exchange for a reasonable prospect of preventing opponents from running up football scores.

They have never done this, in my memory. The hallmark of every one of the Red Sox teams I've watched has been a powerful offensive lineup coupled with a defense at best only so-so. Baseball lore has it that a championship team must be "strong up the middle," teaming a versatile catcher, powerful pitchers, capable people at second and short, and a center fielder who can run like Mercury (because few hitters are dead-pull hitters, at least against major-league pitching, and most would-be hits go through or near the mound, or, worse yet, over it).

Visualize the normal hitting zone this way: fold down your middle and ring fingers of your right hand into your palm. Splay your forefinger and little finger as widely as you can. Think of the vectors thus created as the foul lines leading from home plate, which would be between the first knuckles of your middle and ring fingers. Now open your hand again. Fold down your little finger and your ring finger. Extend and splay your forefinger and middle finger to form a narrower vector. Home plate is now between the first knuckles of those two fingers. The forefinger points to the area between third and short. The middle finger points to the area between first and second base. An imaginary line drawn from between the two knuckles would intersect the pitcher's mound and, at full extension, deep, dead center field.

The majority of batted, fair balls travel either on the ground or through the air in that narrow sector. The melancholy and abrupt decline of Jim Rice provides an instant example: when he was at his best, he could pull the ball in the air, or hit it like a rocket on the ground, into left field.

When he began to lose bat speed, he joined the army of lesser right-handed mortals able only to redirect the ball from its straight approach from the pitcher's mound to the area patrolled by the shortstop between third and second base. Since the majority of players bats right-handed, the shortstop ordinarily puts in the most work—getting the most chances and tallying the most assists—in the course of the usual game, which makes it all the more curious that "most of the parks [built] these days," as Bobby Doerr observed, "favor the left-handed hitters. Fenway was always right-handed, and it's always been one of the few."

Given that, you would expect the second baseman's principal duties would be to police batted balls hit on the ground, or softly into the air, by right-handed batters too weak to pull the ball at all (or by sturdy yeomen batting from the same side against a pitcher with a blinding fastball thwarting all but the luckiest attempts to make full contact and pull it to left), with the rest of his fielding business coming from the left-handed pull-hitting minority who hit the ball on the ground—and you would be right. The second baseman compensates for the comparative strategic immobility of the first baseman, who must stay pretty close to his desk at the office in order to be ready to accept throws from short and third, as well as from second base and the pitcher's mound. So the second baseman, despite the fact that he fields relatively fewer ground balls than his partner at short, needs to be just as agile, to cover the extra ground. And the center fielder, charged not only with the duty of collecting straightaway fly balls hit deep and straightaway fly balls hit shallow, needs wings on his heels and hair-trigger reflexes to capture the hard grounders that skip through the middle.

In the ideal world, those players, occupying four of the thirteen or fourteen defensive spots on the roster (depending on whether nine or ten pitches were carried), would be premier defensive performers. The other nine or ten employed for the rest of protective work in the field would be chosen, if feasible, from the crop of players whose offensive skills are more pronounced.

Clubs are not assembled in the ideal world, not even in rotisserie leagues. Since there are very few young men who can play at major league levels, and fewer still who can excel (Cal Ripkin, Jr., springs to mind) both at demanding defensive positions, such as shortstop, and at the plate, the architects of the teams usually must make choices between those who can hit the ball and those who can throw or catch it. When confronted with those choices, the Red Sox have almost invariably selected those who can hit it, *even when the position to be filled is one of the supercritical defensive four.*

The result has been predictable, I guess: two losses in play-off games; only four AL championships in these forty-two years of my attendance at the struggles; a deficiency of pitching that cost them two World Series; and two more World Series lost on blunders by infielders. Bill James (the *Baseball Abstracts*) has convincingly demonstrated that speed on the base paths is seldom outcome-determinative (as we say in the law). This is *offensive* speed. *Defensive* speed and agility in the outfield, and range in the infield, regularly decide the matter; if the players who enjoy such advantages clip an extra base or two now and then, well, think of that as a bonus. Somebody at Fenway should read that book.

I never knew my mother's father. Roy Montgomery died in Hinesburg, Vermont, shortly after I was born. I suspect we would have gotten along fine, though; he suffered from the same addiction I had caught from Charlie and John.

Roy had been residentially peripatetic, making his wages as an inspector of dairy herds until he was disabled onto a pension by an accident in a granary—a storage unit broke loose and fell on him. Before that, when he was working, he had programmatically diverted part of his salary into the acquisition of distressed farms. He then press-ganged his family—my mother, her brother, Bob, and Roy's wife, Evelyn—into helping him rehabilitate the neglected land and buildings. As soon as the place was shipshape, he sold it for a profit, picked up his family and their traps, and moved to another rundown operation. My mother grew up in: Jericho, Underhill, and Worcester, all in Vermont (where "the snow used to pile so high you couldn't see over the drifts"), and Milford and Hudson, New Hampshire. She did not have an easy childhood, surely nothing like the one that she helped to give me.

Roy was "crazy about baseball." When they lived in Vermont, and his days of disability were long, he would make her drive him twenty-five or thirty miles to Burlington (Bob was in the Army Air Force, as it was then called), saying: "I got to go to the ball game" played between teams of paid minor leaguers, who hoped for the majors, and raw youths, some of them still in school, who hoped to be minor leaguers themselves one day, in a position to elevate their wistful hopes to the next level of the game. Roy endured discomfort to enjoy his obsession; he had to carry a pillow to sit on, and the family disbursing agent, Evelyn, took the same pinched view of baseball that she took of virtually every other aspect of life that I ever saw attract her attention. She disapproved of it, and therefore refused to sanction its observation by allowing Roy money for beer, which she also disapproved of, all by itself. (Evelyn was the model Puritan: if a given activity gave enjoyment to the actor, then it was wrong.) This circumstance neatly middled Doris between the alternatives of enduring her father's plaintive wishes for beer or cadging beer money from a neighboring onlooker (the course she generally ended up taking). She came, understandably, to an active dislike of baseball; it really is remarkable that she chose a husband who would take her out of such servitude in Vermont only on the condition of subjecting her to precisely the same slavery, reinforced by his father (and, soon enough, abetted by her very own son) in Massachusetts. I did not discover this until fairly late in life.

The house at 136 Pacific Street in Rockland where we lived until I was fifteen had five rooms when my parents bought it (my hearsay memory says it cost them $4,500), and only grew to seven when I reached the age and they reached the level of prosperity that required and financed a two-room addition. Until I was about eight or nine, I slept in the bedroom next to the dining room (where Santa still officially put up the Christmas trees). The dining room opened into the living room through an archway, and the acoustics were excellent. Like all prudent children, I eavesdropped industriously as soon as my father finished reading my bedtime story and turned out the light, because when one is small—and when one is larger, too—knowledge is power, and one needs all the power available. By the time I acquired my own bedroom, when the addition was put on, I had developed such acuity at snooping that I could exercise my permit to listen in bed to the adventures of Sherlock Holmes (with Sir John Gielgud as Watson and Sir Ralph Richardson as Holmes) on my little brown Silvertone radio and monitor at the same time parental conversations underway at the other end of the house, mentally tuning Holmes out when a topic came up that seemed to carry implications for me. (It amuses me today when some confident critic of my writing suggests that close study of grand jury transcripts accounts for verisimilitude of fictional dialogue; an only child, billeted without allies among grown-ups, regardless of their apparent *bona fides* and history of loving kindness, operates according to the same sort of procedures improvised by single agents of the French Maquis Resistance, functioning alone behind enemy lines in Occupied Nazi territory, becoming expert at breaking all codes, and remembering everything.)

I recall vividly the night when I was twelve and had been

informed that I had been among those selected for the team sponsored by the Fraternal Order of Eagles in the first season of Little League ever played in Rockland. I was going to have a real gray flannel uniform, and a hat, and spikes, and I was going to play first base. Charlie bought me a new McGregor mitt, a dark brown Ferris Fain model, because I couldn't play first base, after all, with my Mel Parnell model fielder's glove. I basked in his evident pride.

But my mother, it appeared from careful surveillance that night, was a different matter entirely. She had feigned her vicarious delight at the supper table news. Doris, after I was sleeplessly in bed, with undisguised vehemence told John in the living room that she hated baseball, had always hated baseball, regarded game attendance as a waste of time at best and a cruel ordeal at worst, and certainly hoped that he would make the time available to shepherd me alone through the entire adventure and take full charge of it.

I was, in my bedroom, horrified, as shocked and appalled as the politicians say they are when one of their number gets himself indicted. John was calmer. He was unmoved. He said: "I can't do that and you know it. You'd better just get used to it. He's going to play baseball. He's going to go to practice and get his clothes all dirty, and you will have to wash them. He's going to play in games and get his uniform all grass-stained, and you'll have to wash that, too. That's all he's going to talk about, and all you're going to hear, and there's nothing you can do."

I should have done the chivalrous thing and spared her that summer's trial. It would have made points for me with her and saved me from dealing at least that soon with the agonizing fact that I was a lousy player. I didn't make any errors at first base or in right field, at least that I recall (although it would've been pretty tough to make an error, given the charity of the scorers—I think nearly every kid fielded 1.000), but the only times, *the only times*, that I ever got on base that year were by means of walks, or being hit by a pitch, or swinging wildly and fruitlessly at some errant fastball that eluded the catcher while I ran like hell for first. I didn't get one hit. Not one, single, hit.

Ah well, time dims the memory of that tormenting summer, and most of the pain is gone, and time has done some other whimsical things as well: now when the Red Sox succeed, Doris observes in passing that "we" are prospering and truncates telephone calls to catch the games from the beginning. Of course when the Red Sox do badly, I am informed that "your Red Sox" don't seem to know how to catch the ball or appear to have forgotten how to hit it. I guess I am not the only subject of John's hauntings.

The Red Sox, like most teams, generally fare best at home. In '87 the club that finished in fifth place (78–84, .481, 20 games behind Detroit) won 50 and lost 30 in Fenway, playing a creditable 20 wins above .500 ball. On the road they won 28 and lost 54, a dismal 26 games below .500. When they won the Eastern Division championship in 1986, their home record was virtually identical—51–30—but they kept their daubers up on the road, winning eight more than they lost (44–36). The '88 regular season of 89 victories and 73 losses (.549) found them collecting 53 wins at home while losing 26 (.654), but staggering when out of town—36–47 (.444). If they had managed first to extend the American League Championship Play-offs against the Oakland A's to the full seven games allowed (instead of lying doggo and getting swept in four) and had played up to their season record at home and down to it on the road, they would have won 2.61 games of the four scheduled for Fenway, and 1.33 of the three games allocated in Oakland. But as close as that might have been to the necessary best four out of seven—just one break, one little tiny break—it wasn't a likely prospect: Oakland's '88 road record was 50–31 (.618), meaning that on form they stood to win 2.47 of the four projected games at Fenway. And at home the Athletics had an impressive 54–26 (.666) mark that projected them to win two of three games there, giving them on paper, going in, 4.47 wins of the four wins that they needed. And then there was the '88 history of the two play-off teams: at 9–3, the A's had a showy .750 proof of what is likely to happen when one team hits 13 homers in 12 games while the other hits one (Ellis Burks, on August 29th at Oakland).

In '87, as in the previous fourteen years, the American League West (or: Worst, as it was occasionally termed) harbored the pushover teams (not so in '88, when the Red Sox with the same record compiled in the American League Least would have bumbled home in third place). The '87 Minnesota Twins, playing .525 ball (85–77) took the Western Division title, becoming the first team in major league history to win a pennant without scoring as many runs as their opponents did against them. (Which feat they then astoundingly topped by beating the .605 Eastern Division Tigers in the Championship Series as a stretching exercise for their disposal of the Jack Clark-less Cardinals in the World Series.) There was much forced jocularity, disguising chagrin, in such Eastern Division strongholds as Boston that winter, most of it reducible to the proposition that it was ridiculous for a team short of 90 wins to capture the Division flag, but little of it was heard when the Twins met that standard in '88, only to finish second to the A's.

The history of professional major league baseball, according to Pete Palmer in his book, establishes a norm for championship teams; generally they outscore their opponents over the season by about 150 runs.

No Western Division team in 1987 had a winning record

on the road; in the East, Detroit (44–37), Toronto (44–37), and Milwaukee (43–38) finished over .500 games played out of town. Plainly the path to the Eastern Division pennant lay over the recumbent bodies of the Western Division teams. And, just as plainly, the path to the 1988 Western Division title—Oakland finished with 104 wins, while Boston's 89 were sufficient in the American League Least—lay over the supine bodies on the East Coast. Baltimore lost 107 games in 1988.

The Red Sox have found the footing unsure when they have traveled west.

In sixteen years of playing the California Angels, they won 52 and lost 39 in Fenway, but managed only 48 wins against 44 losses on the Wrong Coast. In '87, the Red Sox were only .500 (3–3) against the Angels at home, and pitiably won only one out of six (.167) at Anaheim.

Plagued since 1981 by the vengeful return visits of Carlton Fisk, a sure bet for the Hall of Fame stupidly set free by Boston late in 1980—Fisk still loves to hit in Fenway, the venue of his legendary Sixth Game, twelfth-inning, legendary homer in 1975, and against his old team. He entered 1988 tied for third with Brian Downing on the list of active players with the most homers against Boston: 13 in six years playing for the enemy—Downing needed fourteen years with the White Sox and Angels to do the same amount of damage. Just ahead of them were Eddie Murray of Baltimore (14 in ten years) and Don Baylor, who hit his 17 in fifteen seasons with the Orioles, Athletics, Angels, Yankees, and Brewers. The Red Sox have managed only 47 wins at home against the White Sox, losing 48 since 1972, and when visiting mediocre teams in Chicago have won only five more than they've lost (48–43).

At home they have played the Kansas City Royals to a virtual standoff, winning 45 while losing 43 (the totals, by the way, include strike-interrupted '81; that is why the numbers do not balance out), but suffered prodigiously on the rug in Kansas City, losing 58 while winning only 31.

They split with the Twins at home (3–3) in '72, but won only one out of six in the Homerdome. Things were even—3–3 home, 3–3 road—in '73. They swapped 4–2 home and 2–4 road records with the Twins in '74, feasted 5–1 home and 5–1 road in '74, went 4–2 at home and 3–3 on the road in '75, won 4 at home and 3 in Minnesota in '76, lost 3 games in each park in '77, took all 6 at home and 3 out of 5 on the road in '78, made it 9 out of 12 in '79 (the three losses coming in Minnesota), split again, 3–3 in both parks in '80, lost all 4 at home in '81 (but won 2 out of 3 in Minnesota), went 3–3, 3–3 again in '82, 3–3 and 2–4 in '83, 3–3 and 3–3 in '84, 3–2 and 4–3 in '85, 6–0 and 4–2 in '86, and then in '87 won 5 out of 6 at home while losing 4 out of 6 on the road.

Oakland, in this sorrowful desert, has been a West Coast oasis for Boston over the years, until 1988. Since 1973, when the A's won 5 out of 6 at Fenway, but allowed Boston to play .500 ball on the Coast, the Red Sox have had only two losing seasons against them (4–8 in 1987, 3–3 at Fenway and 1–5 on the road); in '88, when the Red Sox staggered to the pennant 44–40 against the Western Division, they got their clocks cleaned every time they went to Oakland.

They have recorded seven losing seasons with the Rangers: '74, '76, '78 (when they lost all 5 games they played at Arlington), '80 (when they lost 2 out of 6 at Fenway), '81 (when they lost 5 out of 6 in Texas and won only 2 at home), '84, and '85.

The punchless Mariners (except when Stormin' Gorman Thomas was playing for them) in recent years have given the Red Sox no dramatic troubles (Boston held a 36–26 edge at Fenway as '88 began, a 41–23 advantage at Seattle) but have regularly played them tough: the Mariners were .583 against Boston in '87, but finished in fourth place in the West at .481.

In 1987, Boston played 25–17, .595 ball against the West at home, and 13–25, .342 ball on the road against them. Against the tougher Eastern teams, they were .658 at home, 25–13, but on the road they went, 15–29, .341. It all puts one in mind of the preacher's lament: "Lord, we have left undone those things that we ought to have done, and done those things we should not have, and we would like to know why it is that we keep on doing this."

That sort of disparity accounts for Pete Palmer's fascination by the game. Its equilibration of the factors of luck and skill, over the course of the long regular season, is nearly perfect. Johnny Pesky put the same thought in different terms when he noted that the '86 pennant-winning team, which won 95 and lost 66, finishing 5½ games ahead of New York (90–72) in the Eastern Division, took five decisions that year by luck: one victory came in Cleveland when the fog rolled in off Lake Erie (Oil Can Boyd philosophized that such events should be expected when a ballpark is built next to the ocean, another slur on poor Lake Erie); another pair when rainouts rolled scores back to the last complete inning (when the trailing Red Sox had had the lead); one when the winning run was walked home; and another when the winning run was balked home. If four of those contests had gone the other way, the Red Sox would have been 90–71 at the end of the year and been forced to make up the 162nd game, postponed earlier in the year against the Brewers—who clobbered them 1–4 in the five games that were played at Milwaukee. A loss in that makeup game would have put them in a play-off situation against the Yankees; we do not relish such prospects in Boston. In '88, Boston's lack of a practiced first baseman cost the team, by my count, at least four regular-season wins, which is a pretty situation for a team that wins its division by one game.

Palmer, easily losing the mathophobe in the rush of his enthusiasm, said the mean standard of deviation dictates that if each team could begin its next season with the same personnel in the same physical condition it fielded the year before, it could realistically expect either to win or to lose ten more games than it did the previous season (changing personnel, and then managers, midseason, the Red Sox in '88 won eleven more than they had the previous year, but six fewer than they bagged in the '86 pennant season).

In other words, if the '86 pennant-winning assembly had reported for Opening Day in '87 at the same ages, weights, and in the same physical condition that took them to the '86 World Series, they could have been confident only of winning at least 85, while losing 76, if everything went wrong, or winning 105, while losing 56, if everything went right, with the loopers dropping in and the curveballs always breaking. Fasten your seatbelts and make sure your seatbacks and tray tables are in the full upright position, because this is where Palmer takes off.

"Two thirds of the teams should be between seventy-one and ninety-one wins." In '88, six of the teams in the American League East had more than 71 wins, and none had 90. The American League West had four of seven with more than 71 wins: 71 percent, overall. "The mean standard of variation is ten, the square root of the sum of the squares. Six-point-three-six squared times six-point-three-six squared gives a square root of nine, which is exactly what it should be. The variations of skill and chance are about exactly what they should be: even, over a hundred and sixty-two games."

Which explains why the Twins, with their mediocre '87 season, were able to overcome first the Tigers and then the Cardinals, who were probably superior opponents: in a short series the equilibrium of luck and chance is easily broken. In 1985, Kansas City's backup shortstop, Buddy Biancalana, hit .228 and drove in 6 runs in 33 regular-season games, spelling Onix Concepcion (85 games, .282, 23 RBI) and three other journeymen. In 14 play-off and World Series games, he drove in 3 crucial runs, frustrating the Cardinals in 7 games.

This has happened before. Dusty Rhodes batted a creditable .341 for the New York Giants in 1954—principally as a pinch hitter; he started only 37 games—and driving in 50 runs while hitting 15 homers in 154 games (his team won 97 and lost 57). In the World Series, against the 111–43 (still a record) Cleveland Indians, Rhodes in the Giants' 4-game sweep hit .667, drove in 7, hit 2 home runs, and demoralized the opposition that had terrorized the entire American League over the long season.

Baseball is a streaky game; the reason that Joe DiMaggio's 56-game hitting streak remains a record is because it is very hard to get even one hit in four or five tries every day (Dominic managed 34 straight in 1949). Good players maintain top averages by gathering hits in two-for-four or three-for-five clusters. In the brief sieges that determine first the league championships and then world championships, hot streaks of those cluster-hit days and lucky breaks determine very large matters indeed, with the whole world looking on. Doubters are invited to ponder the matter of Jose Canseco, who muscled out 40 homers and stole 40 bases in the '88 regular season, only to become a pitiable, helpless giant against the Dodgers in the World Series, hitting a grand slam in a losing cause and doing nothing in his other eighteen trips to the plate.

Dave Henderson, picked up as backup insurance for the ailing Red Sox outfield in '86—and coming back to haunt them after he made his way to the A's in '88; two of his 24 homers and seven of his 94 RBI were directed against the Red Sox—came from Seattle after 103 games yielding him 14 home runs, 44 RBI's, and a .276 average from 337 times at bat. In 36 regular-season games (four as a pinch hitter) in a Boston uniform, he appeared not to have traveled well: 1 homer, 3 RBI's, and a .196 average for 51 times at bat. The

Red Sox, down 3 games to 1 in the play-offs against the Angels, were trailing 5–4 after a Don Baylor two-run homer in the last of the ninth in Anaheim when Gary Lucas in relief drilled Rich Gedman in the ribs, and Henderson came up next and retaliated with a two-run homer.

Back home in Fenway, Oil Can Boyd (crippled by blood clots en route to what had promised to be a rewarding season in '88) and Roger Clemens threw laughers at the Californians, winning 10–4 and 8–1, setting the stage for the Mets to do the same thing to Boston in the Series.

It works the other way, too. It is safe to say that far fewer observers of Bill Buckner's first seventeen seasons will recall his 1,072 RBI's or his .292 batting average—or, in New England, at least—his 102 RBI's in that pennant-winning season than will bitterly remember the grounder that skittered through his legs in the Sixth Game of that Series and resurrected the Mets for their 8–5 Seventh Game win the next day. (It is also safe to say that few in Boston in '88 cared to remember that Oakland's ace reliever, brother Eckersley, had started on his journey out there as the medium of exchange to the Cubs for that very same Bill Buckner.)

Buckner, of course, like Calvin Schiraldi (the former Met traded to Boston in exchange for Bobby Ojeda), the pitcher shell-shocked by that Sixth Game loss, was thereafter doomed in Fenway. By June 19th of the following year, suffering not only the catcalls of disdainful fans but also the pain of an injured right hip, Buckner was finished in Boston—on July 23rd he was waived and released. (Which fact did not dissuade General Manager Lou Gorman from considering the again-available Buckner as a late-season power pickup from the Royals for Joe Morgan's '88 Red Sox. Morgan, a native New Englander perhaps more aware than the much-traveled Gorman of the intensity and longevity of Red Sox fan grudges, put the kibosh on the notion.) Schiraldi, 8–5, with a 4.41 ERA, went with inconsistent Al Nipper

(11–12, 5.43) to the Cubs the next winter, for reliever Lee Smith. (Postseason heroics were no safe-conduct pass either: Henderson was shipped to the San Francisco Giants on September 1st, his .234 average, 8 home runs, and 25 RBI's good enough only for a player to be named later. That was Randy Kutcher, who showed well in spring training as a general-purpose utility man, but not well enough to make the roster Opening Day.) Boston (63–67 as August '87 ran out) had commenced thinking about '88, and their plethora of hard-hitting young outfielders (Brady Anderson was one of them, but he was swapped out of Pawtucket in midsummer of '88, into the starting lineup for the Orioles in exchange for pitcher Mike Boddicker) were on the doorstep of potential celebration. It is not only teams that suffer from the factor of ill luck; individual players have been ruined by it too.

The team that took the field on Opening Day last year was therefore much changed from the pennant-winning group of '86 and the dismal .481 team of '87. Yet it faced precisely the same mathematical prospects as each of its two immediate predecessors, and all of the others as well. Going 6–4 in its first 10 games (while the Yankees, 9–1, and Cleveland, 9–2, came out smoking), it stood to add or subtract around 9 or 10 wins from its record (78–84) the season before, leaving principally the factor of luck to determine whether that projected 87–75 (or, grim notion, 69–93) would be augmented to 96–66 for contention for the Division championship.

Manager John McNamara had recorded seven losing seasons out of fourteen-plus (he relieved Hank Bauer in Oakland in 1969, with but 13 games to play) in the major leagues. His first three years in Boston yielded .500 (81–81, '85) and fifth place; .590 (95–66, '86) and first place; and .481 (78–84), fifth place again, in '87. He does not misjudge the fly balls, nor does he misplay the grounders, and he dislikes taking action that will reflect adversely upon those responsible. This pattern of behavior reflects admirably upon his personal character. He is a compassionate man who played fourteen years in the minors and compiled a .239 average in 1,120 games, not good enough to get him a shot in the bigs. He plainly sympathizes now with the player who's not quite good enough and affords him every chance to demonstrate he is. But this charity plays the devil with his teams and probably accounts at least in part for his overall record entering 1988—1,005 managerial wins against 1,036 losses (.492). When he departed Fenway Park, he was 1,048–1,078 (.440)—Morgan, in his 77 regular-season games as manager, finished 46–31, went .571 (.569 if you throw in those 4 postseason losses). In the '86 World Series, McNamara knew Buckner was lame, and halt, and feeble in the field. With a lead in the late innings of each of the last 2 games, he should have pulled the man and saved him from humiliation. Jim Rice in '86 hit .324, with 20 home runs and 110 RBI's. His work in the field was very questionable: .977, with eight errors in 354 chances and a lot of charity from the official scorers. In 1987, he had the same .977, but made another eight errors in less than half the chances—171—playing 94 games as opposed to the 156 of the year before.

Rice is a proud man, and he has a right to be: in more than thirteen years with the team, he averaged .302, played 1,898 games, hit 364 home runs, and drove in 1,351 runs. He is an eight-time All-Star. But pride sustains him no better than it did the aging Frank Malzone, whom John disparaged all those years ago. When the '88 season began, Rice was 35, and his knees were shot; rumors of vision problems persisted, intensified by his experiments with contacts and glasses—in the American League play-offs we learned from television announcers that Rice was wearing spectacles around the clubhouse, but doffing them for the games. That general handicap has often been mentioned to explain his habits of charging balls hit over his head, falling back on sinking liners, and his propensity in recent years of popping out and grounding into double plays. (I date Rice's decline to an event that occurred in spring training in 1986, when Peter Gammons of *Sports Illustrated* corralled Wade Boggs, George Brett, and Ted Williams for a free-for-all discussion about hitting. Williams in his customary manner declared that he couldn't understand why American League pitchers continued to allow a certain—unnamed—right-handed slugger to hit around thirty home runs a year when any fool could see he always swung at the first pitch and tried to overpower everything thrown at him when there were men on base. Rice had had 27 homers the year before. He had 20 that season, 13 in '87, and 15 in 135 games in '88.) McNamara in '88 was discernibly reluctant to tell him the truth. He did it, during spring training, but it took him a long time, and much media prodding.

That kind of managerial hesitancy most likely exacerbates the effect of the skill factor on Red Sox season records. The relatively small differences between the records of most competing teams means that thrilling Septembers are available only to teams that have gone diligently about their chores in April and in May. The '88 Red Sox completed their first ten games at 6–4, certainly a workmanlike performance, but when May arrived they began to wander aimlessly through some games, and when McNamara in one of his valedictions at 43–42 for the All-Star break said he was grateful to be a game above .500, he at least was seeing plainly—all too very plainly.

I think the way to look at a team's performance is probably not by counting wins deposited to a team's account; it is by tallying losses debited. At least two of those early April losses resulted from mechanical errors on defense: on Opening Day, Detroit gained its second run on a balk called against Roger Clemens that advanced a runner from first and enabled him to score on the next hit. When Clemens left after nine innings, he therefore took a 3–3 no-decision to the dugout, instead of a 3–2 win. In the tenth, Spike Owen muffed a grounder that should have ended Detroit's inning, giving Alan Trammell the life he needed to hit a two-run homer off Lee Smith in relief for a 5–3 Tiger win. Dwight Evans's failure at first base to end an inning by holding onto a ball thrown to him by Marty Barrett (demonstrating yet afresh McNamara's folly of insisting that the best right-fielder in the league belonged at unfamiliar first) set the stage for another loss.

So, while the Red Sox had played .600 ball, they found themselves trailing the 9–1 Yankees and the 8–2 Indians among Eastern teams with ten games played. It is true that early season streaks can be extremely misleading—the Indians had played several of their games against the Orioles who were en route to 0–18, setting a new American League record for dismal starts. But if Detroit Manager Sparky Anderson was correct (when interviewed at Winter Haven before the last spring game, he said he believed 95 wins would suffice for the Eastern Division winner), the Red Sox ten games into the season had squandered two of the 67 losses they could endure on the way to the pennant. (Anderson was not correct, of course, but then anybody who thinks he knows anything about baseball is almost always wrong.) That left them with a bank of 63 to cushion days when the opposition gets 21 hits and a lead insuperable regardless of Boston's skill in the field or luck at the plate. There will be days and nights as well when bad hops or bad umpiring will cost them victories. (Pesky: "You could say more to an umpire when we played. Now, they're so arrogant, you can't even question their decisions. It's a thankless job, though, and I know that—so long as he doesn't run me [out of the game for

protesting] on a called third strike.") And those unjust out-
comes will be levied against their account just as mercilessly
as the ones they kicked away. After ten games had been
played, Cleveland had a balance of 65 and New York had
66 to meet such grim assessments.

The Florida sun was tropically hot—the steady wind was
fairly cool—and Sam Horn had just interrupted the tranquillity of the occupants of a house perhaps 150 feet beyond
the outfield fence by whacking a batting-practice pitch that
very nearly made it into orbit before coming down on the
roof. Pesky, in his blue warm-up jacket, was leaning on the
rail of the third-base field boxes at Chain O'Lakes Park,
cutting up old touches with spectators of about the same
vintage, when a woman about twenty-three years old sa-
shayed—there is no other word for it—along the aisle that
separates the boxes from the grandstand. She was about five-
ten. Her hair was long and blond, and she wore tight white
jersey pants and white high heels, and a short white jacket
over her white, scoop-necked top. The color of her costume
set off her tan nicely; though the jacket was loose, it did not
entirely obscure the fact that she had large breasts.

Pesky immediately saw his manly duty and called the
attention of us other old geezers to the new arrival. Swift
reckless liberties were taken with creaky neck joints, and
Pesky, whose voice carries, said: "*Hel-lo*, Darlin'." She
paused in her progress and showed a perfect smile. Pesky,
by now entirely aware that he had captured the attention of
the young men working out on the diamond behind him,
conducted negotiations in which he offered to remove his
jacket if she would remove hers. She found that a satisfactory
proposition, and the top proved sleeveless, as well as very
tight. Loud approval was voiced from the geezers, Pesky,
and the players, and this so gratified the woman that she
made her way down to the field boxes and perched on the
back of one, with her feet on the seat, arching her back and

taking the sun, kissing one of the old goats at his request and basking in the admiration of the young millionaires beyond her. One need not be a young man to cherish the game; one of the nicest things about it is the gentle way that it reminds you of what it was like to be eighteen, and have all your teeth.

The same day that the blond distracted the young tycoons practicing at Winter Haven, a somewhat grizzled fellow and I fell into a conversation about the many charms of baseball and the bad ways it has changed. We talked for several minutes about turf and the DH rule, and found ourselves agreeing that the game was played far better before the leagues expanded. I suppose nearly half an hour passed out there in the placid sun before it occurred to either of us that the other seemed familiar. He was Al Bradley, member emeritus in good standing of the newsies' lodge—admission freely granted to all proficient storytellers—and we had not seen each other for a quarter century, when he was a photographer working out of AP's Boston office. Of course we'd had no difficulty striking up a conversation about baseball: we had covered many games together in the press box at Fenway Park, and both of us remembered fondly the excellent seafood Newburg served on toast points in the press room before many of the games—the chicken à la king was also good; it had mushrooms in it.

Neither was it remarkable that each of us had strong ideas about improvements to the game. Everyone of any substance harbors such strong ideas. Vainly seeking to succeed retiring Speaker Thomas P. ("Tip") O'Neill, Jr., as congressman from the Eighth District of Massachusetts, former seminarian Thomas Gallagher in his ill-fated '86 campaign (Joseph P. Kennedy II won the Democratic primary, and thus the general election, going away, as they say at the track) craftily but sincerely strove to make his Democratic Socialist (he prefers "Populist") views more palatable to a lunch-bucket constituency by declaring his firm disapproval of the DH rule. It didn't work, but the sentiment was right. Charlie Higgins in his day believed that Ted Williams should be forced by management to hit to left against the Boudreau Shift. My grandfather could not have known what Williams would reveal to Don Gillis of Channel 5 in Boston nearly forty years thereafter: Williams did not quarrel with Charlie's logic at all; he explained that it took him a long time to learn to go against his natural proclivities, his best abilities, and all his practiced habits, and he just couldn't do it well. He said he tried to respond by inside-outing the ball to left, but that only gave him an inch or so of the bat with which to hit. Then at some sort of reunion he ran into Paul Waner, who in about 20 years in the majors compiled a lifetime batting average of .333 (his best years with the Pirates yielded the gaudy .380 of 1927, the sparkling .362 of 1934, and the stickout .373 of 1936). Waner told him: "Ted, you've got to step back from the plate." Williams laughed. "And after that [the other teams] were just sittin' in the dugout saying: '*Sheesh.*' But eighty-five percent of my hits were from right-center to right." Al Bradley reminded me of Dixie, who also had ideas.

Dixie was a publicity agent who worked out of the North Shore. He wasn't very good at it, and he had a terrible thirst on him. He had a tendency to binge. His wife was aware of both shortcomings and therefore kept him close to home, but every month or so Dixie would come up with an escape plan that required a trip to Boston and a pilgrimage among the seven newspapers—and three wire services—then bunched along Newspaper Row on Washington Street in Boston. Dixie would make his rounds, promoting whatever it was that he had in his satchel, leaving strong men weak with laughter after he departed. When he was finished, he would drink himself into a stupor in McFarlane's, a bar off Pi Alley, which was so named for typesetters, not for mathematicians. (Pied type was the product when a printer in those long-ago days of handset print dropped his tray of lead while he was setting pages.)

Toward the end of World War II, leather of all kinds was scarce, and that applied to the horsehide used to make baseballs. Dixie arrived one day, Al remembered, with a self-described brilliant solution and a bundle of sample goods brought to make his point. "He had this bale of codfish skins," Al said. "He'd been over to Gloucester or someplace, when the fleet came in, and his idea was to cover the baseballs with codfish skins. Well, this was in the afternoon, night shift'd come on, by the time he got to us, and everybody had a good laugh. Dixie took his fish skins out.

"Now it's later that night," Al said, "and I'm going out to lunch with Pete." Another gentle, funny man of our acquaintance who also liked a drink now and then; Pete drank shooters, a shot of Old Thompson rye with a beer chaser, and he'd get three of them back before you could get halfway through a salami on a bulkie and a draft of Bud—the stuff killed him. "We went into McFarlane's, and Dixie was in there, sitting all by himself at a table by the wall, chair up against a radiator. This was February, and it was really cold. So we joined him. And Pete bought him the one Dixie needed to go to sleep on the table. And we had our lunch, and Dixie passed out, and Pete picked up the bale of fish skins and stuffed it behind the radiator, and we went back to work.

"Quitting time comes," Al said. "Pete and I went down to the street, and there's everybody from McFarlane's standing out in the cold on the sidewalk. So Pete, acting innocent, goes up to the barkeep, says: 'The hell's going on?' And the bartender says: 'Dixie died at the table. Nobody wants to touch him.' "

Dixie wasn't dead, of course, and it seems unlikely that baseball will succumb either, as changes less fragrant than his are proposed to improve it. But baseball *has* changed, by no means always for the better, and the serious onlooker deserves to know as exactly as possible what differences those changes have made.

Pete Palmer kindly agreed to enlist as a research consultant for this inquiry, thus lending to it a statistical precision that it otherwise would lack. Because one of my theories is that expansion has diminished the quality of play—by requiring twenty-six teams to dip further into the talent pool than did sixteen teams; by increasing travel fatigue; and by scheduling longer seasons played at each end in colder weather—I asked him to compare the records of five Red Sox teams commencing with the first one that I saw, the '46 club, taking into account no less than twenty-six factors.

The pennant-winning '46 Red Sox played .675 ball, winning 104 and losing 50. Their regular season began April 16th and ended September 29th. They played their final game that year in the World Series in St. Louis on October 15th, winning a total of 107 and losing 54. The regular season lasted 167 days, during which the team traveled about 12,250 miles and had 38 days off. (That's about 23 percent of their work-year; the person who works five days a week out of seven and doesn't fly to do it or spend half the time away from home, enjoys about 26 percent of his or her time off. Of course, that person works between 48 and 52 weeks a year, and few generally cheer, but the travel's still a drag.)

The first league expansion in 1961 was modest enough in terms of teams added. But it was a convulsion in terms of travel. The Philadelphia Athletics had moved to Kansas City back in 1957, but because one city was subtracted and the new venue was in the same northeast orbit (where the St. Louis Browns had remained during their 1954 transformation into the Baltimore Orioles), the amount of travel had been only marginally affected. Now, with the Senators moving to Minnesota to become the Twins (a new gaggle of mediocre ballplayers inherited the old Senators' uniforms, proving twelve victories inferior to the previous undisciplined mob: fifth place, 73–81; tied for tenth place, 61–100) and the Angels perching temporarily in Los Angeles (before moving to Anaheim and becoming the California Angels in '65), there were 16,400 additional miles a year to be traveled, which abruptly more than doubled the grind.

The season became seven days longer, raising the total to 174; the slow demise of the scheduled doubleheader (DiMaggio had had 27 of those to relish in his '46 season) began, down to 21. Six off-days vanished, leaving only 32 among the 174. The number of time zones doubled to four. The Red Sox played 127 games in the eastern time zone, down seven from '46; 27 in the central time zone (five more than in '46), and nine on the Coast.

And another trend appeared, promising the same delights as a good-sized tooth cavity: the '46 Red Sox had a nicely balanced schedule of eight home stands and eight road trips spread over the season, alternating an average of 9.8 games in their baggy white flannels with 9.8 in their baggy gray flannels. (Their shortest home stand was five games; their longest was twenty. Their shortest road trip was three games; their longest that year was seventeen.)

By 1961, though, television had become a budgetary factor of some double consequences. Television to the un-demanding—or parsimonious—fan offered a plausible alternative to the trouble and expense of attending the ball games. Radio hadn't done that; games reported on the radio only whetted visual appetites for the real thing of being there. Baseball management, preferring two cakes to the hard choice of whether to save or to eat only one, had started to ration televised access to home games while generously serving up pictures and accounts of road wars to the loyal fans back home. Those home games that were televised seldom included more than one weekend game, and almost never offered what in advance promised to be a sellout, if the fans were not distracted.

Therefore, since broadcasters and their sponsors were relatively indifferent to the venue of a given game, and because at least in New England baseball management had the upper hand in negotiations, management won that point. And both the trips and home stands shortened for another, related reason: management feared extended road trips would habituate the paying guest to the comforts and econ-omies of staying home to watch the games, while extended home stands would exhaust discretionary income used. for beer and tickets, and thin out the crowds as home stands wore down. They therefore adopted the business principles that have long guided madams managing and recruiting new whorehouse personnel: short bouts of pleasant relaxation in-terspersed with equally short bouts of exciting activity. They teased baseball's customers in much the same manner: they could look in on the delights when the joint wasn't open, but had to pay when it was. Those principles once again proved sound.

So, fifteen years after the Sox lost the Series to the Cardinals, there were fourteen home stands ranging from two to nineteen games (with an average of 5.9), and fourteen road trips ranging from two to fifteen games (also 5.9). And, because the broadcasters and sponsors found more prospects for night baseball than were available during weekdays, the '61 team played 45 percent of its games under lights. The '46 team had spent only 13 percent of its time on the night shift—twenty games. All of those were played on the road. When Charlie and John introduced me to Fenway, the seven tall stanchions were a year away.

Every veteran that I interviewed, except the pitchers, said that both batting and fielding were much more difficult under artificial light, and the pitchers said the hindrance of their defense nullified any advantage they obtained against the hitters. The consensus, I take it, is that seventy-three of the games played by the Red Sox at night in 1961 were probably less proficiently performed than the eighty-nine games played by day.

There is an obvious difficulty in comparing Boston's '61 team to the '46 edition; they were both in the same league, but that was about all they had in common. Gary Geiger played a decent center field, but his .232, 18 homers, and 64 RBI's hardly put him in the class of Dom DiMaggio fifteen years before, who batted .316, with 73 RBI's collected on four homers. Pete Runnels hit a steady .317, driving in 38 with 3 homers in his leadoff spot, and he was nimble around the bag, but Rudy York had contributed 17 homers with a .276 average and driven in 119 batting clean-up for the '46 team. Carl Yastrzemski had promise, but his rookie .266, 11 homers, and 80 RBI's required some patience of those remembering his predecessor in left field—in '46, Williams went .342, 38 homers, 123 RBI's, and even in his 113 games in his retirement season mustered a .316 average, 29 homers, and 72 RBI's. And there are few who would argue that Pinky

Higgins in 1961 managed more shrewdly than Joe Cronin did in 1946.

Still, even deprived of Williams and the Vic Wertz of '60 (.282, 19 homers, 103 RBI's), the '61 edition (76–86, .469) compiled a better record than the 65–89 team of a year before, and stayed at 76–86 the following year. Why, if travel is so tiring? Most likely because the two new teams consisted of fifty players most of whom would not have been in the major leagues without expansion; their combined futilities added 181 new losses to a twelve-team, 162-game schedule previously shared by only ten clubs.

Williams on batting averages: "The first couple years after expansion, the averages go up." So did the number of victories per long-established team: the strong teams gobbled up more than their less-gifted older siblings, but except for hapless Kansas City—eighth in '60 with 58 wins against 96 losses; tied for tenth with the Senators in '61 at 61–100—everybody had at least a snack.

And that was what happened once more in 1969, when the league again expanded—while dividing simultaneously, amoeba fashion. The Seattle Pilots appeared in the West, joined by the nomadic A's, now in Oakland. A new entry was lodged in Kansas City—the Royals. The twelve teams were divided into two divisions. The Royals in the East generously threw 93 new losses into the pot while the new Pilots coughed up 98 (the new Senators, seeming to ripen at the age of eight, finished fourth in the East, winning 86 while losing only 76, but that was a mirage). Detroit (103–59) tallied 12.7 percent of the 809 wins logged by the entire American League that year, and 7.3 percent of the 809 losses, winning the pennant by twelve games. In 1969, the Orioles (109–53) recorded 11.2 percent of the league's 971 wins and 5.4 percent of its 971 defeats, finishing seventeen games ahead of the '68 American League champions. Plainly, in the immediate aftermath of expansion, the equilibrium of luck and skill tilts in favor of the skillful.

The '69 Red Sox logged only 3,350 more miles than its predecessors since 1961—32,000—but started its 177-day season on April 8th, more than a week before Bobby Doerr and his companions began the '46 campaign. Scheduled doubleheaders in part permitted twenty-six days off (15 percent), down another six from the thirty-eight of '46. Now there were only seventy-five day games, eighty-seven under the lights, and the number of games in the most distant time zone doubled to eighteen. Thirteen home stands averaged 6.2 games each, but the range of those stands was only from three to nine. Fourteen road trips averaged 5.8 games per trip, and ranged from three to eleven.

The team finished third in that campaign, playing .537 ball, 87–75, but the Orioles, en route to a 1–4 head-on collision with the Unconscious Mets in the World Series, loped into the league championship, 109–53, nineteen games ahead of the second-place (90–72) Tigers. The Red Sox, in other words, improved their record by only one more win in that season for opportunists than they had recorded when they finished fourth (86–76) to the Tigers the previous year— struggling without Tony Conigliaro (beaned by Chicago's Jack Hamilton late in August of the '67 pennant season after he had hit 20 homers, .287, 67 RBI's) and, for half the season, without Jim Lonborg, whose 22–9, 3.16 ERA in '67 had prompted him to celebrate by going skiing at Vail, where he exploded his knee.

A digression here: The Red Sox gave up too early on Lonborg. It was understandable enough; in '68 he was 6 and 10, with an ERA of 4.29; and his next three seasons—7–11, 4.51 in '69; 4–1, 3.18, in '70 (he started only four games, appearing in relief five times, as he struggled to discard bad habits that he'd developed favoring the knee, thus developing a sore arm [there was at least one precedent for that, too:

Dizzy Dean of the Gashouse Gang ('30–'37) Cardinals (134–75), ruined his arm by changing his motion to favor a broken toe, and in his last five years with the Cubs, and then back with the Cards, won only 16 more, while losing 8]).

Lonborg was 10–7, 4.13 in '71, which correctly suggested his Cy Young '67 had been a career season, but the Red Sox incorrectly inferred that his career was over and swapped him. His next eight years, pitching when at home in bigger ballparks, yielded a better winning percentage (89–72, .552) than his Boston career had produced (68–65, .511). But when his sorrowful Phillie teammates made it out of a morass of last-place finishes into third place in '74, he was 17–13, 3.21. When they finished second in '76, he went 18–10, 3.08.

A note here, and a further digression: Lonborg, when he was going right, threw a vicious low fastball. The umpires in the National League viewed that pitch as a strike much more frequently than did their American League counterparts. Lonborg: "The height of the strike zone was definitely different. You'd have to be from around the middle of the belt down for anything to be called a strike." He explained the varying sizes of the non-Sanforized zone this way: "A lot had to do with the visual perception that the umpire had. In the AL the umpire had his head directly over the catcher's head. And so he wasn't able to see that pitch nearly as well as the umpire in the NL, who had his head to the side of the catcher's head. The AL ump because of his position might have a little more difficulty calling the low strike, because of the perspective. He would miss the pitch down low a lot more than he would miss the pitch up high, just because of that." And why the different positions? "The chest protectors," Lonborg said. "The AL umps wore the big protector then. The NL umps wore the flak jackets. Because of the big protector, the AL umps couldn't get down low like the NL umps could."

Then again, perhaps that's not a digression, because a

good part of the reason for any team's failure to realize its potential often has external causes that the team couldn't possibly have foreseen or controlled. There was Boston's 1969 inability to follow the example of Tammany Hall's George Washington Plunkett—"I seen my opportunities, and I took advantage of 'em." It may be laid to the trade that disrupted the peace of the town and the team as well with the season barely underway. Ken Harrelson, having won the hearts of New Englanders by coming over from the A's (after Tony C. was hurt) to chip in 3 homers and 14 RBI's during twenty games of the '67 pennant drive, had consolidated his grip on those affections during '68, contributing 35 homers, .275, and a team-leading 109 RBI's (he also played 132 games in right field without making an error, and he did it hot-dogging all the way). But the next year, against all odds, local boy Tony C. came back, and the front office deemed Harrelson expendable. Shortly after the season began, he was packaged with Dick Ellsworth (whose son, Steve, made the '88 Opening Day Red Sox staff), 16–7, 3.03 in '68, and Juan Pizzarro, the 6–8, 3.59 reliever, and shipped off to Cleveland. In exchange, Boston got Sonny Siebert, coming off a 12–10, 2.97 '68 season (he won 14 and lost 10, 3.80, for the Sox in '69, while Ellsworth slumped to 6–9, 4.13 with Cleveland), reliever Vicente Romo (he had been 5–3, 1.63 ERA in '68), and the immortal Joe Azcue, who'd caught 97 games, batting .280, with 4 homers and 42 RBI's the year before.

Public reaction to the swap was sulfurously volcanic. Of course the lava also would have flowed if Swampscott's Tony C. had been relegated to the bench, but Red Sox fans have never claimed to be reasonable people—that would be a contradiction in terms. Harrelson, not a ballplayer who happened to have highly developed showmanship instincts but a Barnum who also happened to be an extremely talented and very high-strung ballplayer, followed his nature and emotionally seized the opportunity to grandstand on a cosmic scale. He rewarded his public's outrage by declaring that Boston had irrevocably captured the heart of the boy from Woodruff, South Carolina, one of the few times that Bostonians have heard that sort of declaration from a son of the Confederacy, and probably the only time that most of us believed it. He refused to report to Cleveland, and Commissioner Bowie Kuhn all but had to call out a posse to get the deal completed. Astonishingly enough, Harrelson appeared to have been not only sincere, but veracious, when he vowed he could play his best only in Boston; in 149 games with Cleveland that year he hit 27 of his season 30 homers, averaging .222. He played in only seventeen games in 1970, hit only one homer, and announced he was leaving baseball to see whether his proficiency at golf was of professional quality. It wasn't. He came back in '71 for fifty games, hit 5 homers, drove in 14, batted .199 and called it quits at the age of twenty-nine, a talented man who in nine years and 900 major-league games had hit 131 home runs, 41 of them in his 182 games as a member of the Red Sox. In other words, he played 20 percent of his games for the Red Sox and hit 31 percent of his homers for them. He drove in a total of 421 runs, 131 of them for the Red Sox, again 31 percent of his career production in 20 percent of his games. Of course he got better pitches to hit, surrounded by the dangerous hitters in the Red Sox order, and of course The Wall helped him, but even if his feelings hadn't been hurt by the trade, his career assuredly was.

In retrospect, Harrelson and his loyal legions were absolutely right: even if he had to be sacrificed, the deal was a stinker from the git-go. Azcue appeared in but nineteen games, batting .216, driving in 11, with no homers. Romo, like Siebert, was satisfactory, the nature of his work accounting for the 7–9 won-lost record anomalous against his 3.18 ERA. It's tough for relief pitchers to notch wins; when they do so, they're not succeeding at their usual job—which is holding a lead, or keeping the game close—but allowing the bad guys to tie it up or go ahead, and their teammates get them the win by bailing them out with more runs. What they are supposed to do is get saves, and Romo had eleven of those.

Still the Red Sox *had* to put the courageous Conigliaro back in right field, or Fenway would've been dismantled brick by brick. And he did respond as they had hoped, hitting an astonishing 20 homers and .255, with 82 RBI's, *without the benefit of binocular vision.* (Neither Tony C. nor the Red Sox front office saw fit to publicize the fact that Conigliaro had no sight remaining in his left eye, and had made it back only by dint of iron determination—and hours of practice changing the position of his head when he batted so that he could track the pitch with his right eye; the feeling evidently was that to reveal the Herculean dimensions of the young man's valor, whatever its inspirational value, would be to give opposing pitchers tactical insights that might reduce his triumph. Anyone who has ever tried to hit a pitched ball with vision unimpaired can appreciate what an accomplishment it was.)

And Conigliaro in right field was flanking Reggie Smith in center (.309, 25 homers, 93 RBI's); Yaz was in left, matching shortstop Rico Petrocelli's 40 homers while driving in 111—his average that year was .255; that'll happen when you're going for the downs on every swing. Harrelson probably was expendable, unless, of course, it would have been better to trade slick-fielding but moody George Scott—16 homers, 52 RBI's, .253—and teach "the Hawk" to play first, giving away some on defense, but keeping a lot more firepower (which is what they usually do).

But whatever the merits of the deal, the uproar it caused had to affect the team. It is entirely possible that the extra 3,350 miles they logged that year, the reduction of time off, and all the other factors of expansion, had little to do with the performance that resulted in the firing of '67 pennant-winning manager, Dick Williams, after 153 games had been played.

Major league ballplayers pride themselves on their ability to focus their attention on the field, to concentrate entirely upon the game that's being played. Indeed, they are so relentlessly insistent about this, claiming that messy, nasty divorces, arrests for drunken driving, the antics of flaky teammates, and illnesses in their families do not affect their play, that the listener almost has to conclude they are desperately kidding themselves. Psychiatrists call pathologically extreme cases of such behavior "the defense of massive denial." Red Sox fans regard it as normal behavior; predicting championships every spring, massive denial for us is a natural means of survival. Then, when reality tolls some fresh doom, we do in various ways the same thing that Charlie did, when he slugged the arm of his chair and muttered he'd known all along.

But while we onlookers, most of the time, at least, are not adversely affected in performance on the job when the Red Sox lose, only those with the brains of geraniums can pretend that personal problems exist in different spheres from the ones we inhabit at work and output is not affected. When a close colleague is fired, or uprooted, and replaced by a stranger, at least for a time our ability to perform is diminished, because we become distracted. I am more than willing to concede that professional ballplayers can routinely perform prodigious feats of skill and coordination; I trust they will pardon my polite doubt that they can or do manage to segregate their work on the field from commotions in their lives, regardless of whether the sources of disruptions are personal or professional.

In 1977, the Red Sox provided abundant evidence to suggest that doubt is warranted, and the American League expanded again. Reparations were made to Seattle for baseball's part in the Pilots fiasco: the Mariners were installed. There was also tardy if tacit acknowledgment of the sagacity of the National League's 1969 decision to make baseball international (by franchising the Expos in Montreal): the creation of the Toronto Blue Jays.

The Red Sox traveled 33,600 miles during the 178 days of that tumultuous year, beginning on April 6th and finishing October 4th, hitting 213 homers to lead the league while winning 97 against 64 losses, .602, good enough only for a second-place tie with the Orioles. The Yankees, at 100–62, led by two-and-a-half games with one game left to play, and no one was interested. Boston led the Eastern Division with 859 runs scored (fourth-place Minnesota led the West, and the league, with 867), while allowing 712, well over the 150-run bulge typical of pennant winners. (Baltimore scored only 719 against 653 allowed, but New York had a 180–run margin, 831–651.) Toronto added 107 losses to the season pool for fishing by the established clubs; Seattle gave 98. The Red Sox this time were downright greedy: they took 12 of 13 from the Jays, and 10 of 11 from Seattle. Four Boston players, led by Jim Rice (114 RBI) drove in more than 100 runs. (Butch Hobson had 112, but unfortunately offset that by mauling 23 of his 400 chances at third base into errors, and a fielding average of .946, by far the lowest of any Red Sox regular—that performance deserved to be draped in crepe. George Scott, reacquired from the Brewers after the 1972–73 winter trade, bobbled only 24 chances out of 1,561 at first, fielding .965.)

The team had twenty-seven days off, one more than the '69 club had, but still only 15 percent, during that season. Pitcher Bill Lee appeared to devote most of them to his duties as the acknowledged leader of the Buffalo Heads, making plans for off-field outings and clubhouse frivolities to be carried out by Ferguson Jenkins, Jim Willoughby, and Bernie

Carbo—with, it was rumored, the occasional assistance of Bob Stanley. Though Manager Don Zimmer was not a light-hearted man, he was inclined to be indulgent of hijinks and carousing by his spirited young charges. (Jenkins was the old folks' representative in the group: he was thirty-three, and doubtlessly inclined to cut up some after all his years of running up twenty-win seasons for the Cubs and the Texas Rangers, both of whom he could have sued for nonsupport.)

The reasonable deduction, I suppose, is that the combined effect of personnel problems and the usual lack of pitching—Bill Campbell (13–9) appeared in 69 games that year, notching 31 saves with a 2.96 ERA—probably explains better than anything else why an otherwise good team was not quite good enough. But we Red Sox fans were euphoric that winter: Dennis Eckersley was added to the staff. Jerry Remy looked like the answer at second base. And, to the bilious frustration of George Steinbrenner, our Red Sox had acquired free agent Mike Torrez from the Yankees. "Look," said the Trojans, "those Greeks have given us a lovely wooden horse."

After the war, in 1946, John Redmond left his position as principal of Natick High School to become principal of Hingham High School. He invited my father to come with him, swapping his job as head of the English department in Natick for the same post in Hingham. Then forty, my father found appealing the opportunity to swap an eighty-mile commute for a sixteen-mile round-trip. He transferred intact to Hingham all the enthusiasm that had made him a teacher of genuine excellence.

I have to pause here and produce some evidence, so you will see that statement as one of fact, not merely one of dutiful obeisance by a son to a father who is dead. John had a disposition that was sunny most of the time—not, to be sure, as unfailingly cheering as Charlie's, but then I've never met anyone who could match Charlie for sheer, radiant good will—and he set a standard of fatherhood that I certainly never met. But if he had been a complete stranger with the principles of an Attila in a Gestapo suit, he still would have been a wonderful teacher. It was something that he really *knew* how to do, the sort of intangible gift that some Chinese proverb or other proffers as the explanation for the breathtaking skill of the best horse-trader in the land: he never bothered with the usual meticulous inspections, the hooves, the teeth, the coat, and the cannon bones, but merely stood off a few feet from the beast and studied it, to determine whether it conformed to what he carried in his mind as "the essence of horseness." John knew the essence of literature. He knew it as surely as Ted Williams knows the essence of hitting, and Bobby Orr the essence of hockey. When Orr was playing for the Bruins, I, who knew nothing about hockey and cared less than that, along with thousands of others became entranced, not by the game, which seems rather silly to me to this day, but by watching Orr play it. That was the way John taught English. At least in this republic, such virtuosity dangles before its practitioners no realistic hope of recognition and reward comparable to that which the musical world accords a Luciano Pavarotti, and it didn't in John's day, either, but if it had he would have filled the great halls of this land.

I can recall the day when, to my astonishment, I discovered this. John had left Hingham in the winter of '54–'55 to become principal of Rockland High, during my sophomore year there. It was the title and the damned putative prestige that seduced him, with perhaps more than a smidgeon of "I'll show you guys" for the Hingham School Committee, which had—in his estimation—prejudicially declined to appoint a Catholic, any Catholic, to succeed John Redmond when Redmond became superintendent. As a result, the committee had superciliously dismissed John Higgins's application in particular. Since he was hell-bent for election to take the Rockland job—and Doris always backed him, and I, though certainly brash enough to have asserted an opinion on the matter, had no inklings whatsoever either of his extraordinary skill in the classroom or how confining and exasperating he would find the quotidian administrative duties of the headmaster's office—his ambition met no resistance at home during parliamentary debates over the evening meal.

My English teacher that year was Joe Bell, an enthusiastic and gifted teacher in his early thirties, but subject to the same viral infections as everybody else in clammy New England Februaries. John, six or eight weeks on the job and already becoming restive under its Pecksniffian demands, categorically refused to scout up some babysitting substitute for Joe when illness confined him to bed, and called his own number.

We had started *Our Town*, one of John's favorite vehicles among so many that to catalogue them here would leave no space for baseball matters. Because Joe was a talented teacher, I considered, if I thought about it at all, that we had been making pretty good progress toward understanding what Thornton Wilder had had in mind when he wrote the play. We had not. My father came into that classroom— funny: I was much more uneasy having him as the teacher of my class than I had ever been about becoming the Principal's Son; I guess I feared he would unmask himself as a great fraud and exit to jeering laughter if he grabbed a text in his hands—and within five minutes had us all in his thrall.

You recall how the Stage Manager dominates the play— Hal Holbrook did an excellent job in that role in a public television production some years ago—first directing our attention to the town in general and making us *see* buildings, trees, and lawns, and the church and cemetery that exist only in his mind, then producing other actors, who appear at his bidding, Emily and George and all the rest, and go about their business oblivious to his presence or his control of them, as he predicts their futures. I suppose the natural inclination is to smile, somewhat condescendingly but not contemptuously, at Wilder's insouciant conceit, his effort at a tour de force. Well, that is okay, but as is almost always the case when we patronize a work of skill, it means that we don't really understand what the worker had in mind.

John, assisted by no actors, no lighting—hatless, too (and, for the Stage Manager, the hat and a pipe are important props, required by Wilder's direction)—in that first five minutes had us in our minds out of the classroom and up on the slope above the lake in Peterborough, New Hampshire, the town that Wilder used and the site he had in mind for the cemetery he described. He used only words, a few minimal gestures, an interjected question to us now and then that brought no reply to him because he had us spellbound by discovery of the things we had not seen, or even dreamed about in that play (the location of Grover's Corners, New Hampshire, for example: the Stage Manager gives the co-ordinates as 42 degrees, 40 minutes latitude; 70 degrees, 37 minutes longitude. John referred us to the atlas and we found the spot, somewhere in Baffin Bay, off the west coast of Greenland), and he kept us in that state for the full class period. Then, timing denouement almost perfectly to the bell, he explained the essence of the play to us: "So now you see," he said, "you see: the Stage Manager is God, and that's how he can do these things." And damnit, we did *see*.

If I had been a little sharper, paid the kind of constant attention he was always urging on me, in every situation, I might have gleaned right then and there, and not so many years thereafter, after John had died, what he and Charlie really had in mind in all they did for me. When they took me on family trips, when we argued at the table (as soon as I could talk I had not only full membership privileges at all debates great or small, but also full responsibilities), and when we went to Fenway, they were teaching me to *see*. I suppose I could make some connection here between their unceasing tutelage and the Holy Scriptures that adjure us to be ever watchful, ever vigilant, because He will come like a thief in the night and we'd better have our ducks in a row at all times—they were, after all, devoutly religious men—but I don't think there was one. I think their aims were primarily profane, in the strict denotative sense of the word, and that when Charlie fulminated as the Red Sox stranded runners and we beseeched Vollmer to hit homers, or when John pointed out to me that it was right and proper for Walt Dropo to displace my favorite, Billy Goodman, at first base, because Dropo was a bigger target, a more powerful hitter, and not a utility man at all but a professional first baseman, they were employing baseball as still another laboratory specimen in their relentless program first to teach me how to see, and after that, to think, and maybe understand some of the world a little better. It is all very well and good to aver that the child does not mature until he or she learns to see the universe in a grain of sand, but a grain of sand's a microscopic object of scant interest to a child; a baseball game or *Our Town* is meatier subject matter, something large enough and sufficiently exciting to engage the mind initially and keep it entertained while the process of learning proceeds. Sir Arthur Conan Doyle became so weary of the dismal fawning adoration of his Sherlock that he tried to kill him off, only to be so badgered by Holmes's indignant partisans that he had to plunge his pen again into the swirling waters at the foot of Reichenbach Falls and bring Sherlock back to life. The explanation for that phenomenon, I think, is that Holmes so fascinated readers by his ability to see, and then to think what it must mean, that the stories Doyle had told to entertain had become, without permission, an absorbing seminar. And I think I also know now, some thirty-five years later, why my bedtime was waived when Holmes was on the air.

The pivotal question in almost every human situation, whether fictional or real, business-dull or baseball-thrilling, is: why did he do that? Wilder never declares the actual identity of his laconic Stage Manager. A banker who misapplied close to eight million dollars, causing the bank to fail, did not set down in a memo what he'd done with all the cash, or what had made him do it; that was left to deduction by the examiners of crates of documents, sifting through them one by one, asking as they took each new one: why did he do that? In the late summer of '88, Randy Kutcher one night, inserted as pinch runner, jackrabbited for second on the first pitch thrown to Boggs; Boggs let the pitch go by unhindered, and Kutcher was cut down at second and left to trot back to the dugout with his head down while the hoots and catcalls of the multitude at Fenway Park mocked him. Why on earth had he done that? It was only later that the reason came to light: Joe Morgan had put the hit-and-run on, and Boggs at the very least was supposed to take a swing, at best to hit the ball and drive it through the hole as the second baseman broke to cover second on the steal, the idea being to get Kutcher thus to third. But Boggs airily—and regally; he speaks of himself in third person—explained that while he'd seen the sign "Wade Boggs is not accustomed to swinging at the first pitch." So, Kutcher didn't do it because he is an arrant fool; he did it because he was so ordered, and the nitwit-villain of the piece was Red Sox All-Star Boggs.

In some respects, the Rockland High School John took over in January 1955 resembled the Boudreau-demoralized Red Sox that Mike ("Pinky") Higgins (no kin), inherited that spring. Though abutting Hingham, Rockland was a different sort of town. Hingham was old money and a beautiful Main Street with stately homes and churches set well back behind broad green belts, many of them plaqued with signs identifying them as dwellings dating back to the late eighteenth and early nineteenth centuries. Rockland was mostly no money, with but a few estates surviving from the days when

E. T. Wright had been but one of several shoe companies that had made a few wealthy and allowed most to scrape by.

The people of Hingham who did not send their kids to private schools expected the town's public schools to enforce similar high standards and to brook no insubordination or tolerate back talk. The Rockland kids who did not go to public school went to Holy Family School, and the majority of parents of the kids in public schools were satisfied as long as their mostly unchallenged offspring emerged from twelve—or thirteen or fourteen—years of chiefly warehousing with the paper marked "diploma," which signified conclusion of their childhoods and their adolescent years, their certification as adults, and the full completion of their formal education. John as principal was regularly disparaged by people who would have called him an *elitist*, had that word been within their ken; as it was, they settled for more vulgar terms that quite correctly pegged the dissonance between his aims and those of not only the young folks placed in his charge but also the ones who lodged them there—and, worse yet, harder to bear, many faculty concurred. I don't recall anyone actually employing the phrase, but the dominant attitude among the sullen or discouraged on the faculty was that you can't shine shit, and there's no point in trying.

That morale problem infuriated John. He had spent his years in Natick and Hingham proceeding on the correct assumption that his function was to inculcate in his English classes sufficient breadth and depth of understanding of good writing to enable graduates—barely pausing for breath at high school commencement on their way to four-year schools—to prosper at Yale, and Regis and Smith, at BC and Harvard and MIT, too. His friend John Osterman had operated on the same theory, teaching chemistry, and the teachers of Latin and French, and math and Spanish and history: all of them with few exceptions accepted those enrolled as college students presumptive. In most cases they were right, and the parents and the School Committee backed them down the line. In Rockland, graduating males enlisted in the service or took at most abbreviated tours at vocational schools. The females who had a choice between immediate marriage and some gainful occupation—a fair number did not have a choice, either calculation or miscalculation of ovulations having winnowed their options to one—opted for beautician or dental technician schools. And as most in Hingham were placidly gratified by the results of the collegiate preparation their sons and daughters had completed in the public schools, so most of those in Rockland were perfectly contented with the cul-de-sac conclusions of their children's high school years.

Then there was the matter of money, collected in the form of taxes on real estate. For those young or old who lived in Hingham, with or without children in school, the issue was not how much money was being spent, but how much money was adequate to maintain and improve the excellence of public education. For those who lived in Rockland the issue was how little money would suffice to prevent the enterprise from falling apart. The citizens of Rockland regarded residents of Hingham as snobs, and the citizens of Hingham considered Rockland inhabitants loutish, and a dispassionate observer would have had to conclude that each camp had ample evidence for its views. That same observer would have also concluded that John T. Higgins was about as suitable for principal of Rockland High School as Dwight Evans would later prove to be as a first baseman.

The rivalry was intense in athletic contests between the high schools. Unfortunately for the swaggering denim-clad youth of Rockland, sneering at the affected swells of Hingham, the swells won most of the annual football games and more than held their own at basketball. On the baseball field Hingham creamed us. John's loyalties were severely torn.

Jack Joyce was our coach, and in miniature the attitude problems that John confronted as principal plagued Jack on the diamond. It may be that he had no skill at coaching, but evidence for that deduction was not correctly to be found in our dismal records. Football in the fall was the sport of choice at Rockland High. The best athletes whiled away the winter playing very creditable basketball, but when the snow melted, and the mud dried up, they did not swarm to the baseball field; they went out for track and field. Jack had only ten players available on days when track meets were held. His best pitcher—and hard-hitting catcher—Jack Rinkus, was a topnotch shot-putter, and preferred that to baseball. When Jack McGrath pitched, Coach Joyce had to move Tony Aloisi or John Najarian from short or second to fill Jack's position at third. When Rinkus was putting the shot, Coach Joyce had to substitute Sid Goss behind the plate. He had some good ballplayers, but he didn't have enough of them, especially when the best of them were off doing something else.

That explains how I lettered in baseball all four years of high school. Although Joyce, to his credit, believed that everyone who wanted to play ought to have the chance, there was no way that a batter as inept as I should have played in every game, starting most of them. At least by the standards of the competition that we faced, I was adequate in the field. I was slow afoot, but I had a reasonably good arm, and for what I perhaps wistfully assume to be the same motive that impelled Carl Yastrzemski to excel in the majors, I contrived to compensate for my lack of speed by positioning myself carefully for the hitters. Still, I was a liability at the plate. I went three-for-three *in one game* in my senior year, the only time I ever managed such a feat. All three hits were singles, secured with the assistance of the Middleboro third baseman. He evidently assumed that any left-handed batter—even one batting ninth in the order, which should have told him something—was a dead-pull hitter. In my first at bat I caught him playing back and dumped a bunt down the line. (Bunting I could do. The trouble is that it was one of only three things I could do—I was also good at blousing out my shirt so as to get "hit" by the pitched ball, and I was good at working walks. It's pretty tough to make a career out of bunting after the other side figures it out, greeting each plate appearance by moving the first baseman and the third baseman in to flank the pitcher; it's also humiliating.) But this day the opposing coach must have been dozing. The third baseman, indignant at my trickery, reacted to my second time at bat by coming in close on the grass. I got a change-up slow enough to permit me to loop a soft liner over his head into short left field. The third time I came up, he was wise to my antics, and played back by the bag once again. I bunted again. Joyce sent in a man to run for me at first, "before he gets picked off, congratulating himself." We actually won the damned game. The next night's *Brockton Enterprise* carried the box score. It misspelled my name.

My high school experience proved useful later on. By the time my son was five, and eligible for Farm League of the local Little League, he—not I—was living in Hingham, with his mother and his sister. John spent his first season playing baseball on the same diamond that I had visited for Rockland High. By then the town had long since constructed a new high school; the building where my father had taught had become the junior high (and he'd died seven years before). The groundskeepers in that summer of '74 took a more relaxed attitude toward maintenance than they had during the springtimes of the Fifties; the outfield was blanketed in dandelions, and the grass was long. That last was probably a mercy; the boys lacked basic skills, so that any batted ball within the foul lines was usually a base hit, but the grass at least helped to slow them down so the grounders were triples, not homers.

My first marriage had hit the shoal two years before, but I was still stumbling along in that stage of indecision and denial that's afflicted every person that I know who's gone through such a disaster. The first, and protracted, impulse is to deny the reality of what has happened, and to substitute for it elaborate pretenses that everything is as it was before. It's pretty difficult to maintain such a fiction in the company of people whom one knows rather well, and who are well aware that one's car most nights is not in the garage. I learned a lot in those years; show me any restaurant, movie house, or ballpark, and I will pick out for you the men with the small children exercising rights of visitation. It's like going on dates with your kids, and every time's the first. There is a strained diffidence between the parties, everyone's striving desperately to Have a Good Time, with no room whatsoever for even the slightest disagreement, because Every Minute Counts. Old Dad goes about his parental duties with the same grave demeanor he brings to his job, and the children as well are engaged in serious business, all rightly apprehensive that the strain of the performance will ignite one or the other before the trial is over.

That internal dynamic does not conduce to assertive behavior toward the child's teachers or coaches. The parent is acutely aware that the other adult probably knows the shameful facts about the kid's disrupted home life, and may bring them up if the parent seeks to intervene in the mentor's direction. That will provoke the parent to anger, which in turn will upset the child, so nothing short of molestation will ordinarily suffice to start a confrontation. I did not like the way John's first coaches went about the business of teaching little kids to play ball. I did not approve of their coaching decisions, even when those decisions meant that John played more innings than he would have, had every kid had a chance. I knew exactly why his team had poor morale, and I could see how the discouragement and sadness of the kids who did not play affected those who did, and brought the whole team down. Did that explain why they lost? I thought so then, and I think so now, just as Ted Lepcio believes the Boudreau Red Sox—'52, '53, '54—finished sixth, fourth, and fourth chiefly because Boudreau mismanaged the talent: "I came up in Fifty-two. Took Bobby [Doerr's] place when he retired. Vern Stephens [.300, 22 homers, 78 RBI's in '51] and Pesky [.313, 3 homers, 41 RBI's] were still around. And then Lou apparently got this dream of putting [outfielder] Jimmy Piersall at short. The best flycatcher that ever lived. And they all got pissed off. All I wanted to do was play, without the politics, without getting into the philosophy of the guys that went before. And you couldn't do that then. It was a thrill for me to come to Fenway Park and put on the uniform. Just putting on the uniform. All I wanted to do was play major league baseball. I had very good talent that they didn't use"—he hit 15 homers, .261, with 51 RBI's in 1956, but was used in only 83 games—"and it really seemed like it was too bad." I did not say anything to my son's first coach, but it really seemed too bad.

When John and his sister moved to my house in Milton, in time for his next season, I felt less hesitant. Anxious that among other things he learn to play the game I love so much (and not one whit deterred by the possibility that my inability to play it well might warrant some doubt of my ability to coach it), I found in his new coach, Mel Gondelman, precisely the sort of man that ought to be coaching kids. Mel firmly believed that every kid who turned out should play. More, he believed that every father who was interested should take an active role. His zest was communicable; John in his final year of Little League (Milton Flower Shop sponsored his team) had four coaches. Gil McManus coached the infield. Hugh Putnam was as generous with his advice to the other catchers as he was to his son, Ted, who started most of the games. I worked with the outfielders. Mel oversaw the operation, tutoring pitchers and giving batting advice. We did not allow the kids to throw curve balls; rightly or wrongly we believed that young arms can be damaged by such unnatural motions. Mel was the point man on arguments with umpires, and was forthright as well in disputes with opposing coaches who did not share his easygoing, low-pressure attitude about the games. Every kid played (Joe Morgan did that with the Red Sox in '88, and it worked again). In the gentle evenings of late springs and early summers, John, to my extreme pleasure, proved at second base and on the mound that he had inherited his mother's athletic ability, not mine; he was among several of his team's League All-Stars.

By then, reversing Ted Williams's progress, he was losing his interest in baseball as a participatory sport, shifting his attention to tennis (which in time gave way to squash). If he had continued to play baseball through secondary school and college, would he have developed into a major-league-quality player? Probably not, given the rarity of such raw talent; certainly not, given the degree to which his interest had waned. Still, some of it endures, and the two of us have spent many of our pleasantest hours at Fenway, or in front of the TV at home, criticizing for each other's benefit the performances we see.

With depressing frequency, the '88 Red Sox offered ample chances for such unfavorable analyses. The team that won 14 while losing 6 in April nosedived in May to 11–16, leaving them at 25–22, nicely positioned to drop 4 in a row at home as June began to a Toronto club that had been struggling. Twenty-six of a pennant season's permissible 67 losses had been squandered in 51 games, which meant that the Red Sox, to finish with 95 wins, would have to play .631 ball over the remainder of the season, losing only 41 while winning 70. It is very hard to maintain such a pace over more than four months, and harder still to envision such a turnaround by a team under .500 in early June.

As we saw it, these were major factors in the skid:

Jim Rice at the beginning of the first week in June had yet to hit a home run. After the Toronto series blowout he was batting .244 with three doubles, and a triple among the singles, and only 16 RBI's. With roughly a third of the season gone, he was delivering at a pace that would yield a year's production of 3 home runs and 48 batted in (he finished with 15, 72 RBI's). When Wade Boggs or Mike Greenwell batted ahead of him in the lineup, and there were men on base, opposing pitchers walked them to get at Rice, a considerable insult to a man with 364 career homers. He did not always permit this without a fight, persisting in that habit that Ted Williams had specified to Peter Gammons of *Sports Illustrated* during '86 spring training: swinging at the first pitch. He could no longer deal with a pitch thrown low and away. Almost all of the pitchers, or their coaches, paying more attention than the old Middleboro coach, by '88 had gotten the word. Unless the bases were empty, or there were already two men out, it seemed virtually certain he would cause a double play.

As June began, the brass shook up the team. Sam Horn, useless in the field and unproductive as DH, went back to Pawtucket with Brady Anderson, who'd been clearly rushed into the majors prematurely after only twenty-three games of Triple A experience. Kevin Romine, toting a .358 average with the PawSox, came up to replace Anderson, and Pat Dodson, perhaps just a frustrating smidgeon short of major league ability, took Horn's place. That permitted John McNamara to restore Dwight Evans to right field, which he never should have left, and gave Dodson a desperation shot at making the team at first base. It also required McNamara, at least in his view, to reinstall Rice in left field. Rice bungled two chances on June 4th that the Blue Jays grabbed en route to fashioning a 10–2 victory, and two more on June 5th, when the Jays won 12–4. He charged two balls that he should have played back. He was baffled by the carom effect of the door leading onto the field in the left-field corner, and then threw to the wrong base; that door has been there ever since I've been going to the park, and he'd been contending with it for fourteen years, but it still confounded him.

Dennis Boyd, 5–4, with an ERA of 6.40, and Jeff Sellers, 0–5, 4.96, merely stuck out more than everyone else on the staff as victims of both the team RBI famine and their own inability to preserve leads. The depressing aspect of both of their careers has been their common habit of erasing early, if small, leads in the very next inning or two. Bruce Hurst was 6–3, 3.92, after eleven appearances, having given the Jays 3 homers to put the June 3rd series opener out of reach. Roger Clemens on June 4th was victimized again—his record in thirteen appearances was 8–3, 1.78; it should have been 10–1, with proper defensive support. Lee Smith had two wins and two losses, with eight saves, in seventeen appearances; his 4.50 ERA was sufficient explanation for his .588 percentage of effectiveness (calculated on the theory that he won or saved ten of those seventeen games, which is, after all, what he's expected to do).

The offense scarcely made up for the defensive lapses and the results of pitching inattention. In the June 5th fiasco, Boston had 15 hits against Toronto's 19, but left just as many runners stranded—thirteen. They went into Yankee Stadium with the highest team batting average (.279) in the league, and the lowest number of RBI's (209). They had logged 25 homers. The Yankees had a team batting average of .267, but with 54 homers and other contributions had scored 274 runs and were accordingly up eight games in the lost column. In other words, to finish the rest of the season even, the Yankees could lose 49 games while winning 59 of their remaining 108, playing .547 ball—which is a heck of a lot easier than playing .631, and therefore much more likely. Pesky was only partly right: the simple game can also be extremely hard to watch.

The Yankees cooperated, though, losing 76 and finishing in fifth place. And why did the Yankees tailspin like that? Most thought it was because their abusive owner had so demeaned his players—Don Mattingly, one of Steinbrenner's best, bitterly declared for all to hear that Yankees management thinks it buys with lots of money not only the right to the players' best services, but also their dignity. Morale again: the simple game gets even harder when the wrong emotions stir.

Time in its fine and cruel impartiality showed no mercies to my teammates. Jack Rinkus dropped dead at forty-six of a heart attack at a construction site where he was working. I encountered John Najarian in an elevator in a high-rise office building in Boston about five years ago, and didn't get his name right; in a properly run world, an old first baseman would remember his second baseman–shortstop's name. When I interviewed Dick Radatz, he put me on notice that one of his professional colleagues is Tony Aloisi, and when Tony showed up later to drink coffee with us, I congratulated myself on the prudence that had prompted me to admit to Radatz that I seldom rose to the level of high school mediocrity, playing the game he had played in the majors; Tony was only too happy to provide corroborating testimony. Jack McGrath married my first girl-friend, Kathie Lee Gifford. (The last time I talked to her, after about a quarter century of silence, the principal subject was their divorce.) I haven't seen Jack since 1957.

One of the reasons, I think, that baseball maintains its hold on those it captures young is its reliability, at least compared to life. Life, whatever its transient sweetness, is not reliable. It gets all sideways just when things seem to be in permanent, lasting, contented order. The game is different. If it takes a calendar instead of a clock to record a given contest from start to finish, well, then that's what it takes, and an eager youth is sent to get a calendar. There aren't many human inventions that are that dependable—humans either, for that matter—even though you never know how any one example of baseball will turn out. Old baseball players die, and sometimes young ones too (Tony Conigliaro was betrayed by his heart in 1982, when he was 37; he's been an invalid ever since), and almost everyone is saddened by each new such sharp reminder that the game is not like our individual lives, not even for those who played it. Baseball shields no one, although we pretend it does. Baseball is more like the general life in which they played it and we watched, because it still goes serenely on, uncaring and unaffected, long after they have died.

Those statements do not contradict the terms of the descriptions of the significant alterations baseball has undergone since people of mature years were first attracted to it. In 1988 alone, it endured still another chapter in one thick ledger of peculiar fluctuations; the ball had been covertly doctored over the winter, to reduce the incidence of homers, and when this became evident early in the season, the lords of baseball hemmed and hawed, and then said it wasn't so. Their mendacity on such occasions is more than habitual; as it conveys a certain mild contempt of the snooping media and captious hoi polloi, so it implies as well the fear of all transgressors who suspect with good reason they may have blasphemed, or someone may say they have. The buggers finagle with the ball almost every winter. It is as though the three Weird Sisters had opted for free agency when their contracts with Macbeth came up for renewal, and had made better deals for themselves—low-interest loans; deferred salary payments; promises of front-office jobs, after they retire; incentive payments for weight clauses, All-Star elections, MVP; and all of it guaranteed lest they head out for Japan—with Mammon, brewing forecasts for plunder instead of crowns. But when baseball's nobles are apprehended, they forget their warlock costumes and spin preposterous fancies just like any other sticky, greedy little boys.

Still despite such untender ministrations, the sport continues to retain a general stability that protects the longevity of its appeal. The specialties of track and field that appealed to young athletes like Rinkus have been around since Athens and Sparta were at superpower loggerheads and have attracted their share of partisans. But they have never been more than intermittently profitable to their most proficient competitors. Far more people play and watch what Americans call "soccer" and Europeans term "football" than follow baseball (even today, as its debut as an official competition in the 1992 Olympic Games in Barcelona stimulates interest abroad). It seems likely that professional basketball will become an intercontinental league sport long before baseball's World Series finally achieves the status it has always claimed (although there are Little League fields in plenty in the Low Countries already, most likely installed by American servicemen whose families joined them there, and interest has developed in the indigenous populations; as all contagions carried by armies on the march have shown a way of doing, probably since Julius Caesar was tripartioning old Gaul, certainly since the Crusades).

Still I doubt that any professional sport, anywhere in the world, has a longer record of more lucrative, profitable operation than baseball (unless you count politics as a sport, which was also pretty hard to do in 1988; compared to what national politics had available to headline in that presidential year, the American League East was Mardi Gras in New Orleans; Carnival in Rio; Nashua and Swaps; the Lakers and the Celtics; the bad guys and John Wayne; Fred Astaire and Ginger Rogers, with music by the Boston Symphony, and continuous displays of fireworks), or a better one of accommodation to changing circumstances. Its administrators have dealt, sometimes facilely and sometimes awkwardly, with convulsive changes in technology, demographics, and transportation, and they have diddled with the rules of the game, its equipment, and our credulity in ways that have not always been felicitous, but generally they have made what seemed at the time to be the smallest changes necessary to adapt the game to its age.

So it retains its ancestral symmetry. It is still ninety feet from base to base, still sixty feet, six inches from the pitcher's mound to the plate, and still contested by agile young men whose obvious abilities are more often than not insufficient to overcome the difficulties of the tasks it sets for them—as the same game was for ours, when we played it on a different level. There are not many public institutions that can claim to have weathered the past hundred years with similar grace while remaining recognizable and familiar to a mythical person of years sufficient to recall their origins. The places where we grew up change, and we lose touch with the people whom we knew; they wander off in all directions, as we do ourselves, to deal with their inevitable miseries as best they can while we confront our own, but baseball and the Red Sox remain pretty much the same. This is reassuring as those hairs that don't fall out turn gray, and the kids we coached in Little League complete their college years.

Statistically, though, the game has changed a lot—and vastly for the better, I think. The attentive fan—far less devoted than Pete Palmer, but still actively curious—has access to far more records than he did when I was young. To illustrate: on the morning of June 12th, 1988, about to

149

complete a six-game road trip against the Yankees and the Blue Jays, with an 8–2 victory that would yield a 3–3 record for the trip, the Red Sox had won 27 and lost 29 (.482). They were in fifth place, nine games out. Similar data were available to the partisan of thirty years ago, when a 79–75 team under Pinky Higgins would finish third, despite a mediocre .513 percentage—the Yankees delivered a workmanlike 92–62 season that year, sauntering home ten games in front of the White Sox, thirteen better than Boston.

What were not then available to the chronic follower— the one sufficiently interested in the games to catch most of them on the tube or on radio, plus attending several in person, but not addicted to the point of keeping score of every game at home—were the data that now illuminate much more clearly the explanation for the success or decline of a team, *while it is in the making.* The most casual onlooker on the morning of June 12th did not need Jim Rice's stats (180 at bats in 48 games, .244, no homers, four doubles, one triple, 18 RBI's) to deduce that the erstwhile power hitter was in either the grip of a bodacious slump or the twilight of a productive career (when the opposition routinely walks your third hitter to get at your clean-up man, that fellow has a problem, and they have diagnosed it). But the more serious regular fan benefited from the information, contained in that morning's *Globe*, that the team as a whole was leading the American League in runners left on base (472), averaging 8.42 unrealized opportunities per game. They had gotten a total of 693 runners on base—165 of them by means of walks, hit batsmen, and opposition errors, so those figures showed that Boston was bringing home only 31.9 percent of its possible runs. While Rice was plainly deemed a small threat by opposing pitchers (and rightly so), and certainly reduced the opportunities of the hitters immediately preceding and following him in the order, and while his usual contribution of two or three easy outs every three or four times at bat, not to mention his deplorable tendency to ground into double plays (but that was a team shortcoming, too: the Red Sox, turning 123 of them in '88, undershot their opponents' combined total against them by 40) drastically reduced Boston's percentages of scoring runs, he was clearly not the sole culprit responsible for the lackadaisical showing by a whole team that had come north from Winter Haven apparently loaded for bear. In his previous fourteen years with the Red Sox (including his dreadful '87 tally, when he had 62 RBI's), Rice had averaged 96.5 RBI's per season. Had he continued at that pace through 1988, he would have recorded somewhere between 32 and 33 RBI's by June 12th, only 14 or 15 more than the 18 he could claim just past the one-third mark of the '88 season. (He ended up with 72.)

Rice was, after all, only one of some eighteen players shuttling in and out of McNamara's oft-changing batting order; the entire group had wasted 68 percent of its chances to score, with Evans (38), Greenwell (36) and Barrett (27) the only regulars boasting more than 20 successes. Yet, in seeming paradox, this team, with its maddening habit of discarding scoring chances like so many used facial tissues, at the end of the regular season in 5,545 times at bat had garnered 1,589 hits. Those blows, combined with bases on balls and opposition errors had yielded 813 total runs. That was the best in the league. If only mighty Oakland, running away in the West, really came close (797), then however exasperating Boston's LOB slovenliness may have been to watch, it cannot have been too damaging.

Well, it was. Pete Palmer's statistically grounded rule (that the team that hopes to prevail *should* plan to harvest 150 more runs than any other team in its division or league) was abrogated in the course of that long, sloppy season. If Palmer's maxim is a rough rule of thumb to determine during a pennant race which of the contenders is the plainly superior team (after all, when the race is over, no one needs a yardstick; the unappealable verdict's right there in the final standings), and it is, Boston's patent inability to meet that measure plainly established that the '88 Red Sox were not a clearly superior club but rather one that would win only if all the other clubs took the vapors. And that was exactly what happened in the East, as Boston tumbled home, losing ten of its last eleven and its last three in a row. Detroit, finishing second in the East (88–74, .543, one game out) scored 697, while third-place Milwaukee (87–75, .537) had 674. Unlucky Toronto at 756 total runs trailed Boston in fourth place by only two games (the same as Milwaukee) and 57 total runs. Fifth-place New York (85–76, .526) at 767 was only 46 total runs behind Boston. Sixth-place Cleveland rolled up eight runs in the season's finale against the Red Sox, finishing at 668; the only team in its division that finished more than Palmer's litmus 150 total runs behind Boston's seemingly impressive total was lowly Baltimore, with 547. Yes, the team had honored Walt Hriniak's brave springtime warranty of at least 800 total runs scored, but because it did not score them with average statistical precision—the 813 works out to a hair over 5.00 runs per game—but instead alternated bouts of orgiastic, bulimic, double-digit scoring with excruciating intervals of anorexic one- and two-run losses (they were 19–26 in one-run jousts, 13–16 in those decided by two), it won fifteen fewer games in the 1988 season than its West Coast foe for the play-offs.

What was missing from the lineup was not only Earl Weaver's favorite weapon—the three-run homer; Greenwell would get one, that afternoon—but the lesser extra-base hits. Boston took the field that Sunday with that total of 528 hits, 396 (75 percent) of which had been singles. Those singles are fine for the batting average, and rewarding in runs scored when followed by a solid shot, but the Red Sox had hit into 88 double plays when the sun came up that morning (and turned only 40 themselves), wiping out at least 88 potential runs to add to that horrible 472 LOB. At the end of the year they had stumbled into 163 of those ambushes while bush-whacking their opposition in only 123. Since most double plays demonstrate a team's inability to advance a runner from first with fewer than two out (the reason runners look so stupid when caught too far from the bag to return after a ball in the air has been caught is that either they or their base coaches have in fact been pretty stupid, and the play-ers can expect to get blamed for it), it is fair to assume that Boston spurned about a third more of its potential runs than its opponents cavalierly disdained to score against the Red Sox.

Eight hundred and seventeen of the Red Sox's 1,569 sea-son hits—54 percent—were those lusty singles, which is fine if you've got a dugout teeming with shivering whippets, but a bit frustrating when a panoramic shot of the bench reminds you of nothing quite so much as a well-foddered bunch of senior citizens yawping and rocking on the verandah of a sunny afternoon. For the reliable rescue of slow-moving souls like that, you need the long ball. But, wonder of appalling wonders, the legendary Red Sox powerhouse at 128 team homers in 1988 ranked ninth in the American League, trail-ing even Baltimore (135). The Athletics, looming ahead in the play-offs, had 319 fewer at bats (5,173 men batted for Oakland, 5,492 for Boston) and had hit even more singles (933, or nearly 70 percent of their total hits), but Oakland's 430 extra-base hits included 178 homers—nothing like a nice downtowner to fetch those banjo hitters in—while the Red Sox produced 50 fewer among their 473 extra-base hits. No savvy fan expects the team to capitalize on every chance, but when it wastes an average of ten runners every game—even when it reduces that mean score considerably, as the Red Sox did over the course of the rest of the season—it is being far too charitable.

It is hard to avoid the inference that the well-meaning

but still-responsible villain of this scenario is Walter Hriniak. In twelve years as batting coach, with Yaz's generous plaudits on the record to contradict what one might think of a .253 lifetime hitter (Atlanta and San Diego), no homers, no triples, no doubles—25 singles in a total of 99 at bats in 47 games—as a guru of batting, Hriniak had the leisure to counteract the influence Ted Williams had upon the minor leaguers, and he used it; his charges are the young men playing now (when Hriniak departed, after '88, he was replaced by Richie Hebner. Eighteen years, five clubs, .276, 203 homers, 890 RBI's: at least on paper he looks better).

The issue is not whether a Marty Barrett should swing for the fences every time that he comes up; Barrett is simply not a power hitter, and he is quite right to strive for contact and collect his hits. (He is also plainly as smart, and as mean, and as much a winning schemer in both senses of those words, as a bright-eyed Artful Dodger, full of the Dickens; when he pulls the hidden-ball play, the sneaky zest he cloaks behind an altar boy's demeanor is enough to warm the heart of a juvenile probation cop with two decades on the job, and when his playing days are over—not too soon, I hope—the team that grabs him for its manager will have the envy of the world.) The issue is whether a Wade Boggs, who could be a power hitter—and has been, when he's deigned to alter his swing—should in most instances be playing it safe for his average, when he comes up to bat in one-out situations with at least one man in scoring position. I think the question comports its own answer.

It takes a very long single to score even a fleet base runner from second. Boggs does not hit very many of those, and the flocks of singles that he does accumulate—187 out of 240 hits in his .368 season of '85—yield relatively few runs: 78 RBI's. He hit .357 in 1986; 160 of his 207 hits were singles, driving in 71. In those two years he hit a total of 16 home runs, 89 doubles, and 5 triples. But in 1987, pressed to take

up some of the slack resulting from Rice's diminishing production, he hit 24 homers, along with 40 doubles and 6
triples, reducing his singles production to 130 but driving in
89 runs while still managing to win his third consecutive
batting championship with a .363 average. Obviously this
exhilarating success at combining service to the team with
more private ambitions did not go to his head, though: in
'88 he reverted to form, combing opposing hurlers for 214
hits in 584 at bats (.366, again leading the league) and re-
fusing to be tempted by pitches slightly off the plate (he got
125 walks). Only 56 of those 283 visits to the base paths
continued nonstop beyond first base: he had 45 doubles,
always welcome, 6 triples, and in 155 games hit the same
number of homers (5) recorded by 89-game backup (.249)
shortstop Spike Owen in 257, late-inning, noncrucial, at
bats. (Well, okay, one of them was crucial; it came the day
Joe Morgan taught Jim Rice some manners by calling him
back from the on-deck circle and putting Owen in to hit for
him. Rice designed to have at Morgan in the dugout runway
to the clubhouse, and both had to be restrained, but Morgan
won that passage at arms: Rice got his ass suspended without
pay for three pricey days, and team outlook improved quite
remarkably. For a while, at least.)

It's indisputable that a talented and disciplined man who
invariably bats conservatively—or, more accurately, haugh-
tily and selfishly, if you recall his explanation for that
Kutcher no-hit, no-run humiliation—will collect more base
hits than a talented man who looks to hit it downtown in
emergent circumstances, but it's also indisputable that the
long-ball hitter is more valuable to his team over the course
of the season in terms of run production. To the team the
exchange of 30 singles is a small price to pay for 19 additional
home runs, and 18 more RBI's. To the self-centered player,
who desires to take no chances, it is a different matter. So,
in '88, with Rice deep in a slump that would last until briefly

broken on June 13th (when he hit consecutive two-run homers against the Yankees, apparently so discombobulating Roger Clemens that the Rocket Man allowed fifteen hits and nine runs before he retired in the seventh, down 9–5—Bob Stanley allowed three more before the hideous night was out, and the final was 12–6), Boggs obstinately persisted in his old habits, recording only one homer among 74 hits in his first 209 at bats. His RBI's for 57 games came to 18, projecting to somewhere around 54 for the season. He was admirably consistent, for an imperfect world; he finished with 58. And then Wade Boggs had the common gall to say that if Wade Boggs were batting after Wade Boggs, he'd have more men on base to drive in. Well, Wade Boggs bats first (when he bats first) only once each game, and when he batted third, as he did in the Oakland play-off series, he drove in 1 out of 8—and then said he'd left 5.

This issue has ramifications in other areas considerably upsetting for the manager and coaches. Keep in mind what Jim Lonborg said: early offense makes a lot of difference to a pitcher. He doesn't have to approach each pitch with the precision of a Michelangelo preparing for work on the ceiling of the Sistine Chapel. Given three runs to work with, early in the game, he can rear back and peg it, taking a chance that some ham-and-egger will get lucky. Baseball's adage— "Walks'll kill you"—invites a faulty inference; the bases on balls to weak hitters that precede extra-base hits usually proliferate when the game is very close, *because the game is close*. The pitcher becomes so anxious about keeping the bases clear that he ends by loading them up, and then has to pitch to the slugger, who promptly cleans his clock for him. None of the people whom I interviewed was willing to say that the pitcher's zeal and courage diminish as he watches his teammates strand runners in the early innings, but neither did any deny it. And, by the same token, the enemy hurler has to be heartened as he escapes one disaster after another in the early going, gaining confidence in about the same proportion as his opponent loses it. When Dwight Evans struck out about midway through the last game of the Oakland play-off series in '88, with the bases loaded, it had to improve pitcher Dave Stewart's mood.

John and Charlie, being upright citizens with steady jobs, lacked not only the sort of statistics available to me and my son, but also the sunny benefit of the free-lance writer's trade that allows him to allocate a substantial chunk of twenty months to studying the sport and the data it delivers. Paradoxically, as the Red Sox skidded to 30–32, .484, with a hundred games to play, needing to play .650 ball all the rest of the way to notch the magic 95 wins, I found that my experience had markedly reduced the pain of watching their embarrassments. I think a reasonably careful study of baseball cultivates in the observer the same sort of attitude attributed by my friend Marty Kelly in the medical profession to his colleagues in surgery: "A minor operation is one performed on somebody else." If you know that a .484 team is pretty unlikely to play .650 ball in the next hundred games, you are displeased but not shocked when they drop two in a row to Baltimore, 18–47, .277. If they somehow win the Eastern Division pennant, losing ten of eleven while doing it, you have a better idea of what is coming next, and when it arrives you can at least resume your ordinary daily business without opening your veins.

Charlie, attacking the furniture, was always enraged when the teams that came north in the springtime found themselves in July and August facing impossible challenges in the pennant race, and then failed to overcome them. Even when they were ten games out, with eleven left to play, he expected them to win. As much as he loved the sport, he did not know how to watch the game. I'm not sure I do, either, but I have learned some stuff. Maybe, as John hoped, I am finally learning to see.

I have only one good reason for thinking that it must have
been in the spring of 1948 when Charlie, with John acting
as his bargaining agent, traded the black Studebaker President for the dark blue Olds 98 sedan that served as the
conveyance for Annie's regal Sunday rides. In those days,
faunless, nonnymphed rites of spring for serious males com-
prehended not only celebration of the start of baseball training camp down south (Sarasota, Florida, for most of my
youth), but also the unveilings of new models by the automobile manufacturers, on February 22nd, the real Washington's Birthday (even if it isn't). Charlie and John and I
visited at least a dozen dealers every year, regardless of whether
it was really a buying year. For shivering car fanciers, a new
Cadillac convertible, with great arcing fins, of course, and
buttery leather seats, though parked indoors and quite beyond the realm of purchase possibility was a cheering sight.
And, in years when a new car was "needed" (i.e., John was

itchy), fierce haggling always ended around the first of May because exhaustion threatened.

Doris and I suffered on Annie's rides (except in warm weather, when there was a ball game on the radio; then I at least had some palliative for the boredom, but Doris remained unconsoled). We flanked Annie in the backseat while John at the wheel smoked English Ovals and Charlie rode shotgun, smoking J.A. or Overland cigars. We left the house at 457 Union Street after Sunday dinner, around two o'clock or a bit later, and for the next three or four hours motored south through Plymouth to the Sagamore Bridge, turning westward along the Cape Cod Canal past the Bourne Bridge toward Wareham, then north on Route 58 in Middleboro, passing among the cranberry bogs of Carver.

There one benevolently eccentric grower, Ellis D. Atwood, had applied some of his profits to personal indulgence of his passion for narrow-gauge railroads, buying up and reconstructing roadbeds through his holdings, using the antique rolling stock—freight cars both enclosed and open— and old steam locomotives to deliver the harvest from his bogs to the sorters and baggers in his barns. Word of his installation began to get around, and he found himself offering open-air rides on flatbed cars fitted out with wooden benches. Later, when he spied prospects for profit that he hadn't dreamed of, there came snug little parlor cars with cut-glass lamps and velour cushions, quite competently restored, quite useless for hauling cranberries. A barn was either built or converted to house a station and a refreshment stand, where every imaginable concoction of cranberries— sherberted, ice-creamed, juiced, jellied, cola-ed, candied, and popcorned—became available for purchase by anyone dissatisfied by the natural pucker of the lips. A souvenir stand appeared, and while the visitors chugged through the scrub-pine woods and underbrush surrounding the bogs in the sandy clay of the woods, Atwood's assistants scurried about the parking lot plastering EDAVILLE RAILROAD bumper stickers on every unadorned square foot—bumpers were massive in those days, just as were the cars—of bare chrome, fore and aft and on the corners, if those had been missed by some negligent lad on your last visit.

Feeling the mystical convergence of his avocational obsession by trains and his vocational urging to turn profits rising toward a unitary zenith, Atwood, a sort of understated New England version of Walt Disney, began to build tiny settlements in small clearings along the winding roadbed, putting in small replicas, far too cramped for adult human occupancy, of the spare white churches that dignify New England towns. There were also fake brick banks, and clapboarded general stores, and houses and hotels, even a bar or two. As soon as Eastern Standard Time returned, then in September, Atwood dispersed his cohort through the woods to illuminate those little settlements both within and from without, subtly at first and then more brazenly as the years went by, incorporating Christmas motifs in their window decorations and trimming them with wreaths and greens, so it was nearly always Christmas in the shallow clearings. It was okay in steamy August, but a month after Labor Day any baseball fan who'd missed the signal of the first chilly days of fall got a sharp reminder that the baseball season was indeed over (for in those days, it was), and Christmas the only possibility for delight in sight, until spring came 'round again.

I suppose it was because Doris and I were so glad to get out of that damned car, even for a little while, and because John and Charlie just liked trains (Annie didn't budge from the car for those frolics), that none of us gave much thought to the implications of the fact that the uprooting and conversion of even a narrow-gauge working railroad from genuine service to mundane crop transport, and then to the transient amusement of tourists, all at the whim of a well-to-do bog farmer, suggested something about the future of all train service. It did, though. Sometime shortly after Charlie bought the blue sedan, we began to find it more convenient to ride in it all the way to Fenway Park, abandoning the train from North Abington that had carried me most of the way to my initiation. We traveled to the games we saw in that 96–59, .619, 1948 season in the sybaritically voluptuous frame of mind common to all who could manage again to acquire new cars, now that the war was over. This, we imagined grandly, was how Astors, Rockefellers, Vanderbilts, and that sort went about their rounds from one diversion to another: privately, selective of their companions, slaking importunate thirst with hearty draughts of Coca-Cola gone flat and become tepid no matter how shortly before departure it had been poured into the two-and-one-half quart black Thermos bottle with the red and yellow stripes at its midriff, and the tin cup screwed down on the top.

It's really too bad we don't have brains enough to see what is happening to us when it is something we will find that we really don't like, after it gets finished happening. It would be nice, for example, to rerun the tape of that spring day in '54 when I turned what had until then been an act of mere occasional bravado into an addiction. What I would do is freeze-frame the instant when I lit the Lucky Strike that at last hooked me, erase it forever, and fast-forward the tape up to now, showing me at peace not only with my own better judgment, but in practicing harmony with the credo of C. Everett Koop, Surgeon General. My VCR has lots of controls that I don't claim to understand, but if I could find the one that does that, I would master it in an instant.

But we don't have such foresight. So now when I set out for Fenway Park of a burnished summer evening, I find myself distracted from the coming festival by the necessity of deliberating the magnitude of optional evils. Which is the more disagreeable? To leave my car in a secure garage far enough from the park so that homeward-bound regurgitating fellow celebrants—each of whom has laid down a base of four sausage subs with peppers and onions for what looks to have been at least five quarts of beer—will not find it to puke on, and walk a distance equivalent in air miles to that of the terminal span at Atlanta's Hartsfield Airport? Or to gamble that the damage done to my car in a lot right near the ballpark will be limited to bodywork—which I will certainly not inspect by hand in the dark, having no interest whatsoever in dipping my hands in the urine nocturnally sprayed over it by drunks of stronger stomach—and not immobilize the running gear? I always select the safety-and-take-a-good-hike-for-yourself option, telling myself, but not credibly, that the exercise will carry a bonus of cardiovascular benefits, and that by submitting to it I will escape the postballgame traffic on foot much more quickly and more calmly than I could struggle through it in my car; and besides, think of the savings under my collision damage waiver clause of deductible losses. But that does not eradicate the more-than-mere nostalgic yearning that my memory inspires: I still wish we had those trains. Job in his rue did not get it *exactly* right, but he was fairly close; the reality is just not quite as gloomy as he made it out to be: he that increaseth wisdom doth indeed pretty generally increaseth sorrow.

But not always. There is some happiness to be had from the acquisition of knowledge, and, one hopes, consequent wisdom. When Charlie and John and I rode in the blue Olds to Fenway in the early Fifties, I used to get impatient, along with other casual though devoted fans when such players as Nelson Fox of the White Sox and Peter Runnels, then of the Senators (later of the '58–'62 Red Sox) took forever at the plate, fouling off pitch after pitch. When Fox did it, I concluded that he was a hacker, staying alive by mean subterfuge. When Runnels did it, while still in enemy uniform, I believed it demonstrated his inability to strike the ball squarely, and that he was practicing cheap charlatanry to conceal his pitiable inadequacies. I'm a little better educated now.

When Marty Barrett or Wade Boggs hits an easy grounder or strikes out in the early innings, after taking three balls and hitting five strikes foul, he has caused the opposing pitcher to throw eleven pitches, just to him. That leaves the opponent four pitches with which to obtain the remaining two outs in the inning, if he plans to go nine (which almost never happens now, in this age of The Reliever), and that's seldom enough. It leaves him nine more deliveries if he hopes to go seven, also seldom enough, and if he needs fourteen to record the other two outs, we can plan on him gone in the sixth—120 pitches is about the usual limit now.

Wade Boggs, as he brags, almost never swings at the first pitch, especially in his first time at bat (one of the few aspects of hitting in which he follows Ted Williams's rules— most of the rest of his routine is straight Hriniak). That pitch is often a strike, but it's also one more pitch out of the opposing starter's arm, and an instructional experience for Boggs, giving him a look-see at what he can expect from the pitcher later on. (Why Boggs needs to take extra looks at pitchers late in the season, in the later innings of their appearances, is another matter.) He has his professional shortcomings, but he excels at the espionage aspect of the game, and knowledge is power (though the tuition is pretty steep when its cost is a teammate cut down on a busted hit-and-run, and sends him off the field looking for all the world like the southern end of a northbound horse). When Jim Rice seemed in mid-June of '88 to be emerging from his season's near-total futility at bat, another mirage, one of the first harbingers of hope, arrived when he started laying off the first pitch, thus requiring the opposition to throw him an actual strike instead of anticipating confidently that he would foul off, miss, or ground out any kind of junk. Unfortunately, he soon reverted to his old habits.

Then there is that matter of the importance of striving for a seamless defense, especially up the middle. The pitcher desiring success needs to take an active part in this enterprise. It is not surprising that Clemens and Hurst achieve as they do; in considerable part it is because they field the position capably. Few others on the eleven-man pitching staff carried by the Red Sox in June of '88 could make the same claim. A similar criticism could be made of virtually every other staff whose work I saw that season, and in at least the four or five preceding years. The prevalence of malfeasance and nonfeasance in this area may in fact go back decades; until fairly recently, as I say, I simply didn't notice such lapses, and if a grounder went through the box and into center field, I guess I just assumed that it couldn't have been caught. Well, some of them couldn't, not even knocked down, but a great many of them could have been, and would have, if the pitcher had been tending to business. He should complete his delivery squared to the plate. Left-handers should have the right foot planted; right-handers, the left foot. The glove should be around waist level, ready to pounce on a hot grounder back through the box, or to grab a low liner off the bat. This is Little League stuff. If the pitcher follows through like a man falling out of a tree, and the enemy does not bunt him to death, praise the Lord that Bobby Valentine of the Texas Rangers has not found the time or the inclination to share his insights with his managerial colleagues. When Jeff Sellers got hit on the right hand on the night of June 21st against Cleveland (Sox won, 10–6, on 15 hits, for a three-game series total of 59 hits and 39 runs) and broke the third metacarpal between the knuckle and the palm, it was because, as he told reporters, "I never even saw it. I didn't know where it was until it hit me. Maybe this will wake me up."

He's supposed to know where the ball is, at all times, and at least be prepared to fend it off with his glove; he wasn't. Usually such lapses lead to hot grounders back through the box that either pass unchecked into center field, or are deflected enough to prevent an infielder from making a play; Sellers's broken bone was merely an extreme, if unlucky, result.

Managerial substitutions and tinkerings with batting orders receive much public attention—along with, of course, reports of clubhouse bickering, cliques, and confrontations. We in the media greatly overplay the latter, in my estimation; when feuds break out among a group of two dozen young men, greedy for riches and fame that they had better get early in their careers or will not see at all, anxieties turn to testiness rather rapidly. Furthermore, these spirited animals have no choice but to travel in proximity at least 33,000 miles a year, flying in the same plane, staying at the same hotel, riding in the same buses to meet shared, regimented schedules. Anyone who has ever gone on even the shortest cruising vacation knows how swiftly a big boat becomes a little one, even when the other occupants consist of family or friends whom one ashore holds in highest regard. No one who has taken a ten-day tour, a cruise on a liner, or been part of a convention delegation for even a mere week, ever emerges from the experience without a repertoire of bitter tales about some obnoxious but inescapable SOB, whose disposition and behavior warranted his summary execution, prevented only by the laws of felony.

So, despite the fan's innocent wish that his heroes share—and demonstrate they share—his conviction that they, with him a vicarious participant, are embarked on a sacred mission surely as significant as any undertaken by D'Artagnan and his three sidekicks, no such fraternity exists, nor is it likely to. The Red Sox roster is made up in fact of people often if not always competing as ferociously among themselves as they do as a group against other teams. Add professional jealousies and the usual office politics of such a group dynamic to the requirement that they travel such distances locked up together—try to list twenty-three other people with whom you would choose cheerfully to spend not just your work days but at least half of your waking hours, from April through October—and it's a wonder to me that the clubhouse wars stop at fistfights.

Those continuing vendettas explain much of the turmoil that the media report with such relish. That exploitation in turn feeds the angry frustration experienced by the players removed from the lineup, or not named among the new regulars, when the manager determines to ascertain whether individual changes might not lead to improvements in team performance. The media, at least in Boston, hold not only some of the power to dislodge unsuccessful managers, but also considerable authority over the bargaining positions of players and management at contract time. Ink and airtime are important to Red Sox players, because they are negotiable for currency. The veteran who's removed therefore avoids the deduction that management questions his ability to perform adequately at the job, taking refuge in dour suspicion that his demotion is an act of arbitrary and unwarranted interference with his ambition to retire only when he's rich enough and old enough to decide thus for himself. The newcomer who's overlooked while contemporaries are promoted escapes the deduction that they may be better than he is, by attributing the manager's selection of them to his own principled refusal to kiss ass. The fortunate who find their names on the lineup card do their very best to do no public gloating, making modest statements about the honor of succeeding the veterans, but that best is seldom very good—the ill-concealed high glee is plain; the veterans end up sulking, and the media print that, too.

My point is that I don't think the careful amateur's knowledge of either the constant undertone of snapping and snarling in the clubhouse, or the managerial decisions that temporarily quell three gripers while creating three new ones (and let's admit it: we all keep ourselves well informed about this stuff, because baseball gossip is at least as juicy as any other kind, and everyone likes gossip), is of much assistance when it comes to evaluating the probable performance of the team on the field. A Dwight Evans may not like a Rick Cerone, and resent the devil out of Wade Boggs, but if Evans in right field has a chance to cut down a run at the plate, he will throw the ball hard to Cerone. Or to Boggs, at third. And neither of those gentlemen, whatever his feelings toward Evans, will boot the tag on purpose because Evans will get an assist. These guys are playing for lots of money, money for themselves. They get even more if they win.

What I do think is a fair measure of a manager's contribution is the degree of acumen he displays in accepting or rejecting the advice of his pitching coach. Remember that Dick Radatz, maybe half in jest, distinguished between ballplayers and pitchers. The regular player—an Ellis Burks, say—becomes pretty much a known quantity relatively quickly. If he is a superb defensive player, and he loses one in the lights tonight (which Burks almost never does) or fails to run one down (which Burks never does), a lapse on Sunday afternoon, unless attributable to illness or injury, doesn't deserve much concern from the man making out the lineup card for Monday night. It's the same thing with hitting: a Boggs who has averaged .354 over seven seasons will not be benched on Tuesday if he goes oh-for-four Monday night. It took Jim Rice over a year to play himself out of a job in the field, despite repeated misjudgments, and that is probably as it should be (as infuriating as it is while it is going on).

But those are ballplayers, for most of their careers far likelier than not to perform at about the same level tomorrow as they achieved yesterday. Pitchers are different. Even pitchers don't understand pitchers.

Since nobody understands pitchers, the manager's best guideline is that every healthy pitcher is different, and injured pitchers are incomprehensible. Dave ("Boo") Ferriss was 24 years old, 6′2″, and 208 when he pitched 264²/₃ innings for the Red Sox in 1945—before the team's firepower returned from the service, but also, of course, before the firepower of the other clubs returned as well. His ERA was 2.96. He won 21 and lost 10. In 1946, when the iron was back, he was 25–6, with a 3.25 ERA in 274 innings—an .806 winning percentage in 40 games. In 1947, his arm went dead on him. He appeared in 33 games, but finished 12–11, with a 4.04 ERA, in 218.1 innings. He managed only 7–3, 5.23 ERA in the team's depressing year of 1948, pitching only 115¹/₃ innings in 31 games (9 of them in relief, 5–1, 3 saves), and recorded no decisions after that. He retired after one game in 1950, at the age of 28. In his banner '46 year, in other words, he was good for an average of 6.85 innings per outing (he won one game in relief, and saved three). Two years later, with the defensive and offensive lineups around him virtually unchanged, he could manage only 3.72 innings per outing, nine of them in relief, and his ERA had ballooned from 3.25 to 5.23.

Ferriss is an extreme example of rapid decline, but the syndrome itself is typical: the pitcher in a given game gives early indications, either when he doesn't have it, or when he's losing it. And a given pitcher's career, even when not brutally cut suddenly short by an injury—as were those of Sandy Koufax and Herb Score, to name two—still usually tails off much more precipitously than does that of the everyday player. A hitter can get by for a while on reputation. A fielder, his advancing years costing him a step or two, if he is smart can cheat, and compensate with knowledge of the hitters and the parks. The pitcher can't do that.

Every other defensive position is reactive: the pitcher is the only player on defense who can make a mistake that will lead at once to an enemy run, without the clumsy intervention of an unlucky teammate, because the pitcher can throw a home run. The pitcher can walk the bases full, and then hit a batter, issue another free pass, or heave the ball up against the backstop. The center-fielder, the third baseman, the catcher, the other four players on the field as well: none of them can lose the game on defense, singlehandedly, unless a dangerous situation is first created, and then someone else first throws or hits the ball to him. Then and only then will his negligence, stupidity, inexperience, or sheer lack of talent leave him in the goat's disguise. The pitcher is the only man on the field who can lose any game all by himself.

That is why the pitcher's condition on a given night is so important. If the regular second baseman feels a little gimpy, the first baseman and the shortstop can protect him fairly well; if he feels very lame, the utility man can fill in for him without severe effect. If the pitcher slept uncovered with the air conditioner on, and his shoulder's somewhat stiff, he conceals and favors it at risk of throwing a cream puff to a .220 hitter who doesn't see many, but jumps on the few that show up. It is essential that the pitchers, their coach, and manager, enjoy free and frank disclosure. The measure of a manager is his ability to rotate his pitchers so that none of them wears his arm out—Billy Martin has many faults, along with the rest of us, but the professionally worst of them is not his habit of fighting in saloons: it is his propensity for using pitchers who have told him that their arms are tired, and they're hurt, or need some rest.

On June 23, 1988, Roger Clemens, neatly dressed, accepted an award for his contribution of Fenway tickets worth $25,000 to the Charlestown Boys' and Girls' Club. He told reporters that embattled Manager John McNamara was the best he'd ever seen, and specified that he based his opinion on McNamara's rapport with his pitching staff. On June 24th, Clemens kept to himself the fact that he had a cramp in his right groin, almost certain to demolish his effectiveness, took the mound as scheduled, and yielded six runs to the lowly Orioles in less than three innings. The Red Sox managed two that night. McNamara was gone two weeks later, but Clemens remained secretive with his successor—Joe Morgan. There was something wrong with "The Rocket" in the second half of the season, and he didn't seem to have told anybody what it really was (a cockamamy trial-balloon tale of a mild back strain, incurred moving some furniture at home, was essayed, but didn't float). Sometimes the pitcher takes a loss because his teammates let him down. Other times the pitcher actually does go out there and lose the game. Himself. But he almost always commences that procedure in the clubhouse, before anyone takes the field in actual hostilities. That June 24th outing was one of those games.

So McNamara did not get the bum's rush at the '88 All-Star break because the team was 43 and 42. He got it for what is almost always the reason that managers are discharged: a number of losses disproportionate to talent available, which demonstrate that for whatever irrelevant reason, at least several of the best players have refused to collaborate with the manager and their associates to do whatever it takes to win ball games. McNamara, regardless of his noticeable administrative and personal shortcomings, rejoined the great army of the unemployed for precisely the same reason that he had been conscripted into it before, and if hired again, will be fired again: his players did not care to win.

The layman's virtually irresistible temptation is to analogize such firings to executive dismissals—forced resignations, early retirements, "better offers," "personal reasons"—in government and private business. Indulgence of it probably does no violence to the good order of society, but that doesn't make it correct. The office of baseball manager does not in fact correspond in responsibility, the authority necessary to compel others to cooperate in its fulfillment, or in status and reward to the commercial and professional managerial positions that most of us come to understand either by dealing as subordinates with the people who occupy them, or occupying them ourselves. The chief executive officer for operations in a manufacturing or service company does the same kind of things all day that the counterpart executive (maybe with the same title, perhaps a different one) does in the circus while the show is on the road, or getting ready to go out: he replaces departing personnel, deals with employment contracts, maps marketing strategies, plans distribution, and explains the balance sheet to the stockholders at the annual meeting. The CEO of the circus does not catch, intimidate, and train the lions and the tigers that perform to awe the crowd: that is Gunther Gebel Williams's job. And Williams is the circus officer whose duties, rights, and privileges most—though not completely; there is one big difference—resemble those of baseball managers.

Look at it this way: the one all-but-irrefutable index of relative actual power enjoyed by executives in our society is the company compensation sheet. An outfit can create more titles than the Order of Free Masons, the Knights of Columbus, and the Loyal Order of Moose combined, so that any outsider seeking to find out from the table of organization who can order whom around, and then make it stick, will be utterly bewildered. But the compensation sheet will clear things up in short order: the guy who makes the most in salary and stock options can almost without exception hire and fire the other folks, and what he says will go.

When Joe Morgan had his little runway tussle with Jim Ed Rice in the summer, Morgan was on his way out of an interim agreement into a one-year contract calling for a salary of $190,000. This is not bad for a guy who used to keep himself solvent during the lean New England winter inter-regna of his managerial and coaching assignments with Bos-ton's farm teams by driving a snowplow on the Massachusetts Turnpike, but neither does it place him solidly in command of Rice, reporting for nightly duty in fulfillment of the pen-ultimate year of a contract calling for $2.4 million a year. And that is where the jobs of Gunther Gebel Williams and Joe Morgan are quite different: Williams owns the animals. They perform for him, *in* the circus but not *for* it—after the circus meets *his* demands, not theirs, for what he thinks his show is worth. If you are a white Siberian tiger, as rare as a twenty-game winner with two Cy Young Awards on the shelf, you still had better do what Mr. Williams tells you, or you'll be on short rations and may even find yourself subjected to some corporal punishment. If you are a double Cy Young winner, as rare as a white Siberian tiger, and you don't feel in the mood to do what Mr. Morgan says—say, for example, tell him the truth—you can tell him that you feel good, when you really don't, refuse to miss a turn, and go out and cost the team a game because you feel like it. Morgan doesn't own his beasts.

He therefore has at his sole and discretionary disposal none of the last-resort sanctions available even in these griev-ance-procedural days to corporate and government execu-tives finding themselves in need of punishments or separations of malcontents, malingerers, and incompetents who have balked their wishes. And no other manager has, either; none has since Connie Mack checked out. The best that any major league manager can hope for is that the front office in exigent circumstances will grant his petition to divest the club of one or more players, without compensation in athletic kind, if he deems that the only route to melding a team effective on the field out of an aggregation of two dozen temperamental performers. That is not easy to do, when the grant of such permission will cost the operation $2 million or more in guaranteed wages contractually promised to a fading star (whom no other team will take, given such a contract—let alone trade worthwhile players to acquire the fellow that goes with it).

Because the big-league manager is at the mercy of so many volatile temperaments, housed in so many fragile bodies, self-governed or ungoverned by such a disparate collection of quirky, capricious minds, and because there's not a thing that he can do to change the situation as he schemes and plots and plans to win two games for each he loses, he lacks the indicia of administrative control. Therefore, career profiles of field managers in baseball are virtually meaningless. It's not only the single game that often hinges on plain luck; so do their careers, and their won and lost records.

It consequently follows that it is probably never wise to bet on a baseball team. The adage devised to discourage wagering on boxing—"Never bet on anything that can talk"— according to popular mythology was bitter advice from the lips of a sage who had come by his status the hard way: by betting on a sure winner who disappointed his backers but enriched himself, using his power of speech to negotiate on the side a private prefight agreement with a high roller, betting against himself, and then diving into the tank. I am not suggesting that baseball today's unclean, at least not in that respect; I think the 1919 Black Sox retired that specific sordid trophy for major league baseball for all time. What I am saying is that no enterprise involving luck, manifestly uncontrolled by its chief line officer, and requiring for success eight months of complete cooperation from not one but a whole herd of twenty-four beings that can talk, is a promising vehicle for the onlooker's personal gambling enrichment.

I know whereof I speak, because John taught me well. The first summer of the blue Olds sedan, I became in my ninth year utterly inflamed by the unquenchable assurance that the Red Sox were destined without question to prevail. Even when they finished their ordained 154 games locked dead-even with the Clevelands, I wavered not at all. I was not dismayed when Joe McCarthy chose 4.00 ERA Denny Galehouse (8–7) to defend my heroes' prospects against Boudreau's Bearden (2.43 ERA, 19–7); I knew Boston's Horatio would prevail at the play-off bridge. I shot my big mouth off and refused to heed my elders, and when at last confronted with the upping choice—putting or shutting—I bet a month's allowance (one dollar) on my invincible Red Sox. I lacked experience.

I got a lot that afternoon, and on the four Fridays that followed, when those quarters were withheld until my debt was satisfied. Doris thought John was being cruel, and Charlie slipped me coins. But John was right and they were wrong, and again I'd learned something from him that's stayed with me ever since. And saved me plenty, too. Plenty of cash, that is; like every other Red Sox fan, I've been profligate with sorrows.

We are getting on toward winter here now, just past the climate's hidden seam that joins the end of October to the start of November, north of the meridian slowly raising the Southern Hemisphere into the sun for our winter, tilting us a little deeper into cold and greater darkness every day. The Patriots have been engaged for almost ten weeks now in actual hostilities with their enemies in the National Football League. (At least in the first two-thirds or so of every Patriot season, no game telecast by network from their Sullivan Stadium in Foxboro on a sunny Sabbath is deemed complete until the director has included a long shot of the steeple of the prototypical New England white church in Foxboro center, some miles away, visually warmed by the sprays of gold-tawny, gold-scarlet, and silver-green foliage surrounding it on the lower plains of the Blue Hills. This architectural and natural tranquillity—not the far more common crimson and contorted face of the bundled householder profanely struggling in an equally picturesque landscape of softly falling flakes with a snowblower that won't start—is evidently considered to be quintessentially representative of our corner of the world.) The Patriots this year seem to be in the throes of a peculiar schizophrenia, whaling the bejesus out of teams that have honestly earned international repute for their defensive ferocity, and their offensive program of giving no quarter, then next week tumbling timidly upon their backs and putting all four feet in the air, baring their throats in craven surrender to outfits with records warranting suspicion that they recruited entire starting lineups from the Little Sisters of the Poor. But that is nothing new; it's that way every year. Loretta and I have attended one of their games—they beat the New York Jets, and that was satisfying—and I shall be sure to watch all others shown here on television; that record of personal history will be pretty usual too.

The machine-tooled Celtics are poised but teetering on the brink of another regular season. If Larry Bird's foot problems are cured soon enough, he will most likely lead them blearily—and us drearily—through eighty or so games that don't mean much, as the price of yet more play-off rematches between them and the Detroit Pistons, or them and the Chicago Bulls, or them and the Milwaukee Bucks, or them and some upstart other club, the name of which slips my mind right now, in order that, if all goes well both for them and the Lakers, things will again come to the sort of denouement reportedly held most fitting: another championship confrontation between Larry Bird and Magic Johnson. If Bird's feet don't recover fast enough from surgery, Magic will have to play alone. Either way, it will be exciting, and I will be sure to tune in.

When, as and if that happens, and all has gone right, or at least acceptably, for the Bruins as well, in the course of their more pugilistic but surely quite-as-drearily long regular season in the National Hockey League, the strong boys in the Boston Garden will be celebrating the arrival of the vernal equinox by melting ice this morning to put parquet down for tonight, and taking parquet up again tomorrow afternoon so that they can freeze the rink beneath for the next night's Stanley Cup game. Chances are I won't attend one Bruins game this year, and probably won't even watch them on the tube. Bobby Orr back in the Sixties first attracted my attention to that most perplexing amalgam of Ice Capades and what looks to be a sack race version of fifteen tag-team rounds of boxing for the light-heavyweight championship of the world, primarily I guess because Orr pretty much stuck to playing what looked like a real game and was too quick-silvered on his skates to get punched very often. But mine was a fickle attachment; when Orr was banished to the Chicago Blackhawks, which left them instead of the Jacobs brothers and their Emprise Corporation to meet the high cost of harboring not only an aging superstar, but his by then unreliable knees, my fealty deliquesced and leaked away like crystals of salt vanishing on a humid, still, New England afternoon in August.

And anyway, I will have enough on my mind then, in June, because along with keeping a benign weather eye on the Celtics and their fortunes, if any, I will have been for more than three months once again engaged, with my son, and most of our friends and acquaintances, in the supervisory duties that occupy far more of New England's hours of potential profit than good solid management would ever countenance (assuming, of course, that good solid management in New England enjoyed such a choice, and the ability to enforce its provident decisions, which it doesn't). It is good to pay respectful and supportive attention to the Patriots and their strivings when the sinews of the winter are just beginning to appear beneath what lingers of the leafy sleekness that comes with the summertimes. And it is similarly right and just, as the first snows begin to spit down on the unraked leaves, to confer conversational accolades upon the prodigious feats accomplished by Bird, Kevin McHale, and the forbidding Robert Parish, with the self-effacing generalship of Dennis Johnson, the ex-Blue Jay, Danny Ainge, and this year's magic rookie, pilfered neatly on a low draft-pick by larcenous Red Auerbach. It would be proper too, if I had more time that I didn't need to work, to utter a kind word or two for Terry O'Reilly's fighting Bruins, but I haven't, so I won't. Only the man born into wealthy independence and a life of twenty-six-hour days, eight-day weeks, and fourteen-month years (or acquiring those gifts in later years by becoming a sports agent-lawyer) can hope to accord full and due attention to all of the sports and all of the sportsmen, often in full cry all at the same time, in this deceptively scenic, reputedly restrained, veritable Klondike of athletic riches. (And before someone reminds me: yes, I know I am not even mentioning the panoply of amateur sports, from Marathon to Beanpot Tourney, and all the other regularly scheduled college sports as well; you anticipate my point.)

A man in his middle years, when the kids are either pointing toward college, going through college (and making ominous noises about plans for graduate studies), or emerging from college trailing trains of horrid debts, simply can't afford to have more than one real sports obsession. This is true, I have no doubt, in San Francisco and Topeka, Laramie and Houston, St. Paul and Miami, and every other town and city between sea and shining sea, regardless of whether there happens to be a local professional team fit subject for such absorption. (When there isn't, if tales of Texas high school football, Indiana high school basketball, and high school hockey waged in the Iron Range hamlets along the Great Lakes are to be believed, the bereft layman somehow makes do.) I am certainly in no position eristically to argue that all would be better off if none suffered an obsession, because I don't think that's so—for one thing, the passion's fun, and that will do quite nicely for the other thing as well. But contradiction in terms or no, the reasonable and prudent man must be held by kin and friends to become and remain aware of the gravity of the real world, the rise and fall of dollars, the spending habits of his household, and so make progress in his years. One obsession, only one, is appropriate and feasible, and merits single-minded maintenance, once it has been chosen.

I keep busy during the winter months. Things are nowhere near as hectic as they start to become soon after mid-February—when the equipment vans pull out of Fenway, headed south, and pitchers and catchers report—but there is activity.

There are trades to be deliberated across the meat case and in the back room at the Milton Food Market; Mike, Bill, and Al long since ratified my judgment—if it was mine; Mike may have reached it first—that Rice's bolus of a contract must be swallowed and the frustrated ex-basher set free. Mike Mone, over one of our regular lunches at the Locke Ober Cafe, years ago reported with mixed amusement and vexation that his son had become livid at Yastrzemski, correctly deducing that left field belonged to Yaz as long as he cared to patrol it, which meant that young Jim Ed Rice, whom the boy greatly admired and considered a far more dangerous hitter, would be unjustly deprived of the opportunity he deserved to play full-time until Captain Carl stopped acting like a slow dog in the manger. "What can I say?" Mike said. "He doesn't remember Sixty-seven; he wasn't even born."

There are lineup changes to be pondered. When Marty Kelly duked me with a ticket to Fenway one night when Stanley was starting, I found myself appointed counsel to defend the pitcher against a psychiatrist's charges of pathological professional instability, and I'm not sure that either Stanley's sterling effort that night—he pitched a symmetrical

3–1 Red Sox win—or my eloquence won him a lasting acquittal.

There are personnel shifts to be debated. Dick Manley, drawing upon years of estimating personalities and characters from his position as a legislative watchdog of the Massachusetts General Court, and a keen observer too of Commonwealth executives, endorses the Mercer-Higgins proposal to trade Boggs and "Oil Can" Boyd to New York for third baseman Mike Pagliarulo and Don Mattingly. But, like Leslie Epstein of the Boston University faculty, he thinks that even though Yankees owner George Steinbrenner has impeccable credentials as a most impulsive fellow, he is unlikely to become so superheated at Mattingly's lèse-majesté public remarks as to trade him away to the Red Sox. Leslie proposes a more modest effort: Boggs for Pagliarulo, straight up, but that does not appeal to me; as much as Boggs annoys me, he should bring more than that on the open market. (My son doesn't think he should bring anything, except the rest of his playing days to Fenway, and defends this position by calling Boggs what he indisputably is: the best pure hitter right now practicing baseball, "and you shouldn't trade the best." That's a hard point to beat down.)

And there is speculation to be done. When Joe Palingo delivers the heating oil with dismaying frequency during the cold months, the OPEC cartel's depredations and, more recently, its woes, come in for due comment, but then there are more important matters to discuss, such as whether there is any real prospect that the farm system will have produced a capable southpaw reliever by the time the crocuses appear in March.

The aspect of all this talk and disputation that most exasperates eavesdropping laymen, and unwilling family listeners, is the same one that so nourishes active contributors and their aiders and abetters: there is no end to it. The season doesn't suspend the baseball chatter from the wings off the stage where fall and winter sports are giving their perfor-mances; the baseball talk is muted some, but one needn't really strain to hear the muttering. And those who monitor it, very much against their will, know what's going to happen when the ducks fly north again. The trades that really did get made won't quell the back-and-forth; if we disapproved of them, and they haven't turned out well, we have that to talk about. If we clamored for them, it will not matter in the slightest how they balance out; one way or the other we will find cause for complaint. It never, never ends, all this Red Sox argle-bargle, and in a world where so much does, that is no small comfort.

Even when there's no one around that you know, and not much really to talk about, there's always someone around, and something to talk about. I didn't go into the Brattle Street Bookstore in July of '88 for a baseball book; I happened to be on West Street in Boston and dropped in to see if I could replace a copy of A. M. Sperber's biography of Edward R. Murrow (entitled, appropriately enough: *Murrow*), an admirable book absent from my library without leave. In-quiries of the clerk (confirming that the Brattle didn't have the volume, as my own search had made me fear) overlapped the arrival of a stranger, gray-bearded like myself, but crowned with a Mets cap. This seemed to call for comment, this being Boston and all, and that the infidel's emblem. He was forth-right. He admitted to being an '86 turncoat, saying he'd deserted when the Red Sox that year reached and exceeded the limit of his ability to endure pain, but said he was think-ing about reratting (as Winston Churchill denominated his act of rejoining the political party he had departed years before) in order to cast his lot with Toronto. When I asked him to explain how he could entertain such a notion, given the Jays' failure to that date to vindicate preseason predic-tions of their certain eminence (and they persisted, too, right to the end of the season), he did so in one sentence: "Jimmy

Key got hurt. It's still better for my heart and soul than following the Red Sox."

If that chap stays in New England, he has chosen for himself, I think, a path of desolate, mute wanderings down through his remaining decades. No matter where he goes, whether on an evening stroll among the catwalks of the yacht basin in Nantucket Harbor, out for Sunday dinner at a small inn in Vermont, down to the fish market near the water at Ogunquit, or into a gas station hard by Tanglewood, he will hear in those places, and in traffic jams all over from the radios in cars stuck in lanes adjoining his, the same laconic badinage from Coleman and Castiglione that will assault him in the drugstore. If he wants the island sunset, he gets the Red Sox with it. If he wants Chateaubriand, fine; the Red Sox come with that. A little night music, sir? Absolutely. New England can supply it—with, of course, the Red Sox. A long day at the office? The Red Sox will see you home. If he stops in a bar for a cold beer, he will get pictures, too, and every word and every image will reconfirm for him the fact that he's in worse shape than even pitiless S. T. Coleridge dared inflict upon his Ancient Mariner. Because, you see, here in New England, no gray-bearded loon detaining wedding guests, mingling with K-Mart shoppers, even stopping one of three at random from the oil-sodden throng of passersby on the boardwalk at the Rhode Island State beach at Misquamicut, ever gets a chance to say what story will be told. That has been decided. When the Sox are playing, we have our albatross.

This winter I and fellow conferees considered, most assuredly not for the first time, and most likely not for the last, familiar but persisting problems needing prompt attention. Tops on my agenda, as you might have expected, was the item of wasted chances. During the '88 regular season the Red Sox left 1,269 on base—7.08 per game. Their opposition left 1,121—6.90. Boston won 19 games decided by one run, and lost 26; they lost 16 two-run games while win-

ning only 13. In other words: though they had 14 shutout victories against 13 shutout losses, they were 32–42 in close games—nearly 58 percent of their 73 losses; around 36 percent of their 89 wins—where those stranded runners would have made the difference.

Part of the explanation certainly lies in the difficulties the Red Sox have when they play on artificial turf. Another part surely lies in the strange power outage they had; even though they won 53 and lost only 28 at Fenway, a premier hitters' ballpark, they were out-homered on the season, 68–73. (If Boggs, with five, had matched his '87 production—24 out of the park—that deficiency would have been reversed, and he would have been much closer to driving in the 89 runs he produced in '87.) And much of the reason for the team's futility in close games sits in the bullpen.

Joe Morgan, working his '88 magic, was afraid to use lefty Tom Bolton at the horrendous (1 win, 10 losses) end of the season. Small wonder: Bolton was 1–3, 4.75 in 30 innings, allowing 16 runs. Stanley, used primarily as a set-up man for Lee Smith, went 6–4, 3.19, but he gave up six homers in nearly 102 innings pitched in 57 appearances. Marty Kelly's irritation was not without cause: the enemy on those occasions scored 36 runs. And Smith wasn't blameless, either; in less than 84 innings, he gave up seven homers among the 72 hits he allowed.

True, fastball pitchers are homer-prone—Roger Clemens served up 17 in 264 innings; when the occasional batter gets around on a ball coming at him around 92 miles per hour, it tends to go a long way—but when relief pitchers throw them they come at the worst possible times, in games in which the Red Sox have left eight or nine on base, and are therefore more rancidly memorable, like the smell of good meat that was not broiled in time, but allowed to go bad in the fridge. It cannot have been lost on the Red Sox front office that the contemporary strategy of handling starting pitchers calls for them to work usually five days after their last appearances—it used to be four—and retires them after seven innings' labor; that is almost certainly why there are fewer twenty-game winners now, even though there are more (weak) teams and eight more games to be started. That is why the bullpen is so important, and also why it is essential to build the biggest possible lead as early as possible—by reducing the LOB rate and thus giving the relief man the leeway to make his one big mistake, without losing the game, by himself.

It seems to me that a number of things have to be done to accomplish that. The first is to insist—here we are again, back to what Dick Radatz said about the basics—that the protocols of base running be inculcated in promising young players before they arrive at Fenway. Everyone, in every line of work, makes mistakes, but those who survive in their trades soon learn not to commit them at crucial times. It is infuriating when a runner ignores the third-base coach and either runs through a STOP sign or fails to heed it—and equally infuriating when the third-base coach misreads the play and gives the wrong sign. It is not easy to get a runner to third base—or to second, for that matter—and it is foolish to waste his potential score.

When there are fewer than two outs, it is essential that the man with the bat in his hands know how to bunt. On the '88 roster, Marty Barrett knew how to do it, and so did Jody Reed; Ellis Burks had an inkling, but it seemed to escape him as the season wore on, and the rest of the team, with the possible exception of Spike Owen, appeared to regard the operation with haughty disdain. I think the reason was that the majority in the starting lineup correctly believed that they were not fast enough to make a hit out of a bunt and were so mercenarily mindful of the bargaining power batting average statistics provide when contract time arrives that they simply refused to do it. But those refusals meant

the runners were not advanced, and when the hitter failed—
as Boston hitters did that year, 72 percent of the time; they
had a .283 team batting average in '88—the chance of scoring
the runners diminished dramatically. And what resulted was:
LOB.

The simple game gets harder as you get older, and it's
much more difficult to tolerate the selfishness that has come
to dominate it since free agency became a fact. This is no
brief for the sort of owner domination that characterized it
when I was a kid. I belong to a union, too—the Writers'
Guild of America—-and have to fill out the forms and send
in the checks just like everybody else. I know the players
have short careers—much longer than pro football's average
of two and one-half years or so, but still short—and I know
those careers aren't easy, but I also know those careers now
pay handsomely while they are in progress, and I pay the
going price to watch those players have them. It seems to
me that what they ought to do is exert every energy to win,
and they don't always seem to do that.

Maybe it was better when you couldn't see it coming, the
way you could in '86, when they blew the Sixth Game of the
World Series to the Mets, and the way you could in '88,
when they staggered backward into the Eastern Division title
and then turned out flat as flounders for the opening game
against the Athletics at Fenway. When John and Charlie and
I went to Fenway in '53 in John's red and gray Oldsmobile
98 Holiday (Lord, but *that* was a beautiful car) to watch Mel
Parnell (21–8, 3.06 ERA) or Mickey McDermott (18–10, 3.01
ERA) pitch (but not Ted Williams hit—he was flying over
Korea, and Hoot Evers, .240, 11 homers, 31 RBI's, was
playing in left), the imminence of disaster was not so ap-
parent. Not that it didn't happen—they finished 84–69, in
fourth place, 16 games behind the Yankees, 99–52, with
Ellis Kinder picking up 27 saves. It was just that hope abided
longer, and hope is the Love Potion No. 9 of the Red Sox

fan, hallucinogenic, maybe, but still an absolute essential.

In the spring of '82, I was, not for the first time, under the mistaken impression that I had some profitable business to transact in the shark-infested waters of Hollywood. It seemed to Loretta and me an opportune chance for Susan and John to inspect Southern California and view all the exotic animals allowed to roam free there (those residing at the San Diego Zoo are indisputably the most attractive and least dangerous).

After I had been disabused, by means of much silken abuse, of my newest naive belief, and they had seen all the zoos, we fetched up in a house in Palm Desert, near Palm Springs. It was loaned to us by the Dodger partisan who had shown us them at work (his name is Matt Byrne; he does something or other for the federal government out there). It was hotter than the clabbers of Hell in the desert, and the midday sun enforced a noon curfew on tennis. (None of our small band commits golf, which, I gather, is the principal cultural activity out there, as well it might be: people who appear at least to have had large amounts of money to spend on fairly luxurious quarters seem to find nothing incongruous about living like pocket rajahs in homes on Lawrence Welk Drive. Most peculiar, I think, but then, they have no Emersons, Hawthornes, or Longfellows, and must scrabble cachet where they can.) That left the pool near Matt's house, for those who like that sort of thing, and the television as a refuge for those who get their fill of pools quite fast. The College World Series was on, and when son John came in from the pool I called his attention to a sizeable young fellow throwing what appeared to be white BBs at terror-stricken opponents of his University of Texas Longhorn team. John and I concurred: it was really too bad that the Red Sox never drafted and signed human bazookas like that lad.

When it was time to close the house, I drove up the road to get a gift of wine for our host. The clerk in the liquor store was a medium-size gentleman with thinning black hair, eyeglasses, an attitude of helpful courtesy, and an air of extraordinary animation only barely under control. He made several valuable suggestions for my selection and small talk about my accent—many out there find it very singular indeed, quite different from their uncultivated mode of pronouncing the mother tongue—and what we had done for fun. He asked whether we had taken in any of the spring training games being played by the California Angels up the road, and I said that we had not—I had been unable to assemble from our bare quorum a working coalition willing to get all dressed in order to sit somewhere else in the sun, with no pool nearby for quick cool-offs. "Besides," I said, "I'm afraid I might see Fred Lynn"—he was playing for the Angels then—"and since I'm on vacation, I don't want to get that mad."

The clerk's agitation grew. I surmised aloud that he might be a baseball nut as well. That did it. His eyes shone behind the glasses, and the joy seething within him bubbled out in words. He was indeed a baseball fan, and had been afflicted all his conscious life, but now he was much more than that, with still more yet to come. "My son's in the majors," he said. "You ever hear of Bud Black?" There isn't much future in lying to real baseball fans, not about baseball, at least, so I knew there couldn't be any at all in lying, however kindly meant, to a real ballplayer's father. I admitted I had not. "Well, you wouldn't've," he said, in his happiness disposed to be charitable toward everybody in the world, even those who talk funny. "He was up for a while with Seattle last year, only pitched in a couple of games. But he got traded, over the winter, over to Kansas City. Now he's got a real chance, and it looks like he's on his way."

As a matter of fact, young Harry Ralston Black, then twenty-five, did have some very creditable games stored up in his young arm; if in the hot desert that day I had possessed the powers of Thornton Wilder's Stage Manager, I would have told that jubilant proud father that the Royals in but two short seasons would assemble enough winners and luck on their squad to win the Western Division Championship, and that the best pitcher on that staff would be Bud Black, 17–12, 3.12.

But then, I suppose, he would have made me tell him what else I knew, and I would have had to sadden him by disclosing that the Tigers would sweep the Royals 3–0 in the then best-of-five championship series, and that his son would give up all the runs Detroit would need—two, in the 8–1 decision, and that Bud was destined after that disappointment for seasons of 10–15, 4.33 in '85; 2–10, though 3.20, in '86; 8–6, 3.60, in '87; and, after KC traded him to Cleveland, 4–4, 5.01, in '88. I wouldn't have liked doing that.

So, nearly forty years later, I understand why my father, teaching *Our Town* to my high school sophomore class, made such a point of Wilder's omission of all evident emotions, except mild pity mixed with puzzled sadness, from the Stage Manager's comments on the *tableaux vivants* he summons up to show (as Emily discovers when she comes back from the dead for one more precious day of life on this blessed earth) how we ordinary people in our ordinary days miss so much as they go by, and never even see. And also why the Stage Manager always wears the hat (the other players are behatted only when they go "out"); He is out there all the time, watching over them.

Well, anyway: I of course congratulated the liquor store clerk, and said I wished his son, Bud, every possible success except when he pitched in Fenway Park, or the Red Sox came to watch him and his mates play on their rug. The man's happiness that day was proof against all brashness. "You know," he said, "you're the second person, talks like you do, I had this conversation with. Guy came in the store last week. Said exactly the same thing."

The young Texas pitcher that we saw on television out there worked obscurely the two seasons that the Royals needed to provide the backup Bud Black needed. But after '84 was underway, John and I saw him again, along with that scorching fastball. We saw him at Fenway Park. His name was Roger Clemens.

C harlie was buried in Latin. My father ordered him laid out in the front room. If you've ever wondered why you have not been invited to sit in the front parlor of a lace-curtained Irish house, it was not because its owners wished to insult you; it was because they had no corpse on hand that day to display in the room and therefore scrupled to permit not only you but family members, too, entry into it. (If, on the other hand, you find bowls of fruit in such a house and no one there is sick, you have a right to feel aggrieved; they most likely have two toilets, too, and in place of fragile lace, actual draperies. God only knows what they actually use that front room for, certainly not for the wakes—they use the funeral home for those.)

After the bitter-enders had left on both nights (evening calling hours are traditionally seven to nine, but no self-respecting person of Irish descent ever left a home wake until at least ten-thirty, even in a temperance household—you never can tell: there's always a bite to eat, offered after nine-thirty, and someone might serve a free drink; it would be a shame to miss that—which is one of the more persuasive reasons for using the funeral homes), my father enlisted friends to maintain the watch all night—John Osterman; Bill Coughlin (an attorney from Abington who served with John and Charlie on the bank's board of directors); Bill Lynch, who had taught math with John at Hingham High; I think John's boyhood chum, Father Dan Flavin, may have been there too, home from his mission parish somewhere out near Bismarck, North Dakota. (Those were palmy days for the Church then, when men like Father Dan came late in life—he had been in the shoe business—to their vocations. The Archdiocese of Boston had no parishes for them, and dispensed them generously to trackless wastes that had none.)

This was another manifestation of the Irish tendency to carry all things to extremes; whatever body-snatching outrages the Auld Sod's rowdy boys had perpetrated back in Ireland, the odds against such raids at 457 Union Street in Rockland, Massachusetts, in 1955, were extremely slim, and the self-denial of needed sleep by the chief mourner was a needless exacerbation of what is almost always a marrow-exhausting trial. John did it anyway. Doris and I told him that he was being foolish, and it did no good at all. Then in September 1966, when John lay in state in Charlie's place, I, of course, did precisely the same thing.

The biologists assure us that ontogeny recapitulates phylogeny, the vertebrate embryo, for example, developing at term into human form only after passing through phases of unmistakable resemblance to the lower forms of animals with backbones. Well, filiogeny (don't bother looking it up because it's not in the dictionary; I am coining this word here because we need one to describe the *postpartum* process of development that causes a male child to repeat, more or less faithfully, the stages that his father went through as he became a recognizable though imperfect copy—variorum, perhaps?—of the new son's grandfather) recapitulates patriogeny (I am this, too). It does so inexorably, regardless of whether either of the generations wills it or recoils in horror from it, so that if you scrutinize very carefully the character and usual behavior of any man whose father was around during his boyhood, even if your subject insists that he loathed his sire, and cites abundant reasons, sooner or later in his inflection of his speech, some unthinking gesture or spontaneous reaction, smart or asinine, you will see his predecessor, the gleeful old bastard, grinning back there in the shadows, pretending that he always meant for it to happen, when the chances are he almost never thought of it at all. That is why the scions of Red Sox fans become Red Sox fans in their turn, regardless of their complete awareness that it's a foolhardy thing to do, certain to bring torment; they are imprinted from birth (as are, every so often, certain unlucky female offspring, the get of truly advanced sufferers).

It was hot late September when Charlie's two-day vigil was held, four years to the month after Annie's wake (she'd been in the front room, too). Mourners whom I did not know lined up in twos on the sidewalk, shaded by the turning leaves on Charlie's three big maples (one of which has gone since he did, its roots killed by a gas leak), sometimes so many of them that the line stretched up beyond Lena Barry's house, four up the street from us, the one next to the church.

I was fifteen when Charlie died in 1955, and certainly quite as stunned as John or Doris was. The brain defends its capacity to function despite undeniable logic of inevitable sorrows drawing closer day by day, by compartmentalizing the facts that would prompt sad syllogizings. My grandfather was eighty-one. Eight or ten years before he had had what all except he termed "a real bad heart attack." I had not then, nor have I since, ever met or heard of anyone whose heart attack was "good"; a friend of mine, Jim Krumsiek, had when he was forty-five what he called a "mild heart attack," but less than a year later, when he had the one that killed him, I learned that Jim had rather brazenly understated what had happened that first time. Not that Jim's was my first experience in being lied to on such matters; when Charlie was hospitalized, and then confined to bed at home, he minimized the reason. By the time he was allowed to get dressed so he could fidget in a lawn chair on the back porch, concealing if not quelling his displeasures with the Red Sox as reported by radio, a person overhearing him describe his health to me would have sworn the hearty fellow had been arbitrarily immobilized for no good reason by timid idiots with medical degrees who had enlisted my tyrannical parents into enforcing their damned rules. The way he talked about it, I ranked that heart attack about equivalent in discomfort, and cause for concern about his future, to what he would have suffered if he'd failed to turn a light on when he'd retired for the night, and so stubbed a toe or barked a shin on the bedpost: it was nothing serious.

Because I wanted it to be just that, nothing serious, I propagandized John and Doris just as he had planned. Sooner than he'd been supposed to, he was once more up and doing. I've forgotten now how long he had been ordered not to leave the house, and then how long he'd been restricted first to two hours, every other day, and then two every day, and then a half a day each day, and so on by gradual progression, carefully monitored, until everything seemed safe enough, if it ever did, to allow him to resume his ordinary schedule as the treasurer of the Rockland Cooperative Bank. What I have not forgotten is that he tackled the prescribed intervals in a sort of methodically negative, logarithmic way: he took all of the bed rest, half of the sitting rest, a quarter of the alternate-day, two-hour shifts, an eighth of the daily two-hour shifts, a sixteenth or so of the half-day shifts, and then pronounced himself cured, one hundred percent fully fit, in just the terms a banker would use: "I feel like a million dollars."

For quite a long time I guess I was the only one of us, except of course Charlie himself, whom he really had deceived about what had happened to him. But Doris and John, though much more skeptical, were pushed beyond their ability to disbelieve by the undiminished vigor that he showed. Annie had died at her own pace. She had broken a hip several years before, and had been querulously and demandingly bedridden; she knew what was appropriate behavior for old people hurt or sick, even if her husband didn't. She spent those years browbeating muscular, live-in practical nurses (one of them stole from her jewel case, another was utterly nuts, but the last was a female bruiser with the good nature of a heavyweight boxer, who took no abuse from Annie or others because she so clearly would brook none) four days a week. Doris suffered it on Thursdays and weekends when the nurses were off. Then Doris's mother, Evelyn, moved down to keep his house in the winter, and we shuttled each spring and each fall between Pacific Street and his place. No complaints of health or temperament were voiced by either Charlie or Evelyn, and after a year or three, I guess, John and Doris had acceded to their own wishes to believe Charlie immortal, or at least indestructible, just as he claimed to be.

That was why the three of us, and Evelyn, too, later were rendered all but incapable of more than perfunctory speech when the duty nurse on the morning shift at the Lynn General Hospital told us he had died while we were having breakfast. The myth of durability he had built around himself had been pretty well nigh shattered by the heart attack he'd suffered the previous evening at the annual dinner of Massachusetts Cooperative Bankers—at the New Ocean House in Swampscott, it too gone these many years—and John had not before that confined to inflammatory ball game situations his misgivings that his father in his ninth decade might not be quite strong enough to put in full days at the bank, and then pile such things as fifty-mile rides and banquets on top of them. But still, when we got the news that this man of eighty-one had died, we were thunderstruck, and in that state we did remain, on automatic pilot, until the funeral was over and our reasoning brains kicked in again.

Charlie would most likely have taken the more pragmatic view he invariably expressed at wakes of persons over sixty, to all of their bereaved: "Seventy-two, eh?" he would say. "Well, he had no kick coming."

The mourners who stood in the sunshine thought they had one, though. My father and mother stood in the front room, among banks of cloying, stinking, allergenic flowers that all but hid the bronze casket and nearly Charlie, too, composed beneath the roses. My hay fever dispatched me to greet callers in the screened sunporch, so-called with supreme illogic because it was shaded by its roof and the tall maples, and ask them to sign the guestbook before they proceeded in for the viewing and the prayers. I was not only ignorant of most of their names, which slightly rattled me because he'd shown me off repeatedly to many friends and I thought I knew them all, but also of what made them come, a lot of them in tears.

I had better luck getting their motives than I did securing their names, either from their quivering lips or from the signatures they scrawled. These were the people who had financed their first—and in most cases, their present—small homes through the Cooperative Bank, either before the Depression had struck the economy as a whole, or before it hit them later, on a delayed-action fuse. They had contracted to pay not only mortgage principal and interest but annual town real estate taxes as well in monthly installments to the bank. Out of work, their savings mostly gone into down payments, they had found themselves fearfully addressing two now-dreaded officers at once, when destitution struck and they went to the bank to face ruin.

One of those officers was Charlie Higgins, who had in many cases rammed their somewhat shaky applications through to full bank board approval, and the other was Charles J. Higgins, moonlighting not only as town tax assessor but as town tax collector as well. Today, of course, in our improved society of enlightened vigilance, not to mention puffed-up civic sanctimony, laws against conflicts of interest prohibit such comminglings of private and public trusts; if Charlie got caught doing that in the late 1980s, even though his books were straight, he would find himself, at one hundred and fourteen-plus years of charitable age, first being sternly lectured by some senior jurist seventy years his junior and then being escorted down to the House in Plymouth County where Correction is provided. But if he were alive now, and he did now what he *did* in those offices back then, as those real mourners told me, taking oaths with every tear, Charles J. Higgins would go straight to the Massachusetts Correctional Institution at Cedar Junction, in manacles and leg chains, and for a good long stretch of damned hard time. It's not only baseball that's changed.

It sounded, as they told it to me, one after another, in different words and poor syntax, like the kind of stories that you hear today from survivors of our disasters, almost incoherent repetitions of peril, despair, and then, when all seemed absolutely lost, the rescuers that saved them in their terror. They all told the same story. I will compress it once here, from what so many said. "I lost my job. I couldn't get another one. We used up all our money, and the wife tried to get some work. We cut down on everything, but it seemed like nothing helped. They shut off the electric light. We couldn't get no heat, and finally it got cold and we had to pay those things, and then we didn't have the house money, and we went up to the bank. And we talked to Charlie

Higgins and we said we couldn't pay, and we knew he didn't want to but he'd have to throw us out. And he said we shouldn't worry. He said: 'We won't take your house. We know you'll pay up when you can. Go home and don't worry.' Charlie Higgins saved my house," and when the times improved again, they saw Charlie and paid up. And Charlie portioned out the money honestly between his bank and his town, and even though a lot of Rockland people were destroyed by that Depression that ate lives like a wild, ravening animal, a lot of people who knew Charlie somehow made it through. When he died, decades after his unilateral and high-handed suspension of mortgage and tax foreclosure laws had at least prevented the wolf from getting into the living quarters after it broke through the door, they remembered well enough to demonstrate that the respect he'd had for them was returned in theirs for him.

I am not particularly proud of the response that I improvised to deal with those heartfelt stories. In our small family, effusions of emotion were kept to a minimum and made everyone uncomfortable when they rarely were indulged. Now I found myself not only trying to deal with my grandfather's death, but also apparently called upon to comfort total strangers who seemed to be worse off for it than I was. I had command of wits enough only for a few hasty perceptions. I knew that I did not know what the hell to say to these devastated callers. I dimly recognized that I was genuinely angry at them both for making such sloppy spectacles of themselves, and for intruding upon my own sorrow, which surely outranked theirs (ah, the only child again, ceaselessly charting hierarchies of entitlements, placing his own at the top, and bridling if all whose needs he has ranked farther down fail to accede peacefully). And I guess that I was apprehensive that in my weakened state I lacked full command of the verbal weaponry of sarcasm that I have always called upon when I feel at all threatened. I needed a distraction, and I needed one damned fast, some soothing reassurance that beyond the metes and bounds of our lawn, and the line of grieving visitors, and the six more hours of the wake, the funeral and the funeral luncheon, there yet remained a world in which good order still prevailed, and things remained just as they were, and Charlie had not died.

The Dodgers were en route to beating the Yankees, four games to three, in the Series. I went into the front room, where Charlie was laid out, and asked my father if it would be all right if I turned on the ball game on the sunporch radio, and he interrupted his handshaking and gestured at the casket and said: "I don't think he'd mind. I think that's what he'd do." So that is what I did. The mourners came. The mourners went. When they signed the guestbook, they heard the baseball game. When they said their last farewells, they heard the play-by-play. Some of them, to be sure, inquired after the score, and made a brief prediction of the eventual result (most of them picked the Yankees, and grimaced doing it; we Red Sox followers know what generally happens when the Yankees smell the cash). Most of them, especially the older women, looked openly askance; my deed caused quite a lot of talk, little of it favorable. But that was not my first time as a local scandal-giver; when I was about six I had rather boldly tried out the notion of addressing my parents by their Christian names. (I got it from a *Saturday Evening Post* story about a little kid whom I now see to have been offered not as model for the bright tyke I then assumed he was, but as a prime exemplar of obnoxious little brat.) Neither John nor Doris saw any hint of turpitude in this, and on the theory that those after all were in fact their names, encouraged me to do it. More than once I was chided by some shocked family friend, and several times by adults who pumped gasoline or worked in restaurants, and overheard such usage. Their firm view was that I was committing disrespect of parents, and they were seldom shaken in it by

Doris's or John's rejoinder that they did not feel disrespected and would be much obliged if the correcting volunteers confined their performance of disciplinary offices to their own family circles. At least one member of the Rockland High faculty expressed dismay when I called the new principal by his first name, stating apprehension that this would lead to erosion of school discipline. John riposted mildly that he hardly thought it practical to make me call him "Mister," and assured the affronted lady that while he allowed me to do that, and also to drive his car, he did not contemplate general extension of such privileges to the entire student body. People got upset about trivial matters in those days. Maybe it was because they had no drug problem to concern them, and the only incurable sexual affliction was unwed motherhood (which was seldom mentioned in a voice above a whisper, but the whispers did abound).

The priest who celebrated the Mass of Requiem for Charles J. Higgins that bright autumn morning four days after he died wore a black chasuble with the crucifix chased in silver thread on the front and on the back. The large congregation viewed chiefly the cross on his back as he moved about the altar, saying and singing the consecrating prayers, the altar boys responding to most of them in the same hard *c* Church Latin, the congregation seemly murmuring, in that same dead language, those few oral contributions we were called upon to make. The Second Vatican Council was seven years away. If in 1955, in the bowels of St. Peter's Basilica, or the Curia warrens above, furtive monsigniori were even then carrying out clandestine, cryptic directives, none of us had even a clue. If amanuenses in black vestments were surreptitiously on paper constructing philosophical scaffolding for liturgical demolition experts in deep-cover training at Louvain, or other scattered depots, we had no inkling of it. The Epistle and the Gospel were delivered by the priest, from the pulpit, over Charles J. Higgins, and there were no other major dealings done in English until the ceremonies neared their end. Then all of us, kneeling, in English called upon the Blessed Virgin to intercede with God in behalf of her servant, Charles, who had departed from us, and also upon Our Lord Jesus Christ, to have mercy on the soul who had shown so much to others. Standing, we repeated those importunities outdoors at the grave. And that was all of it. If you had told John or Charlie, in 1955, that the day was not far off when Roman Catholic laymen in this bright country would yammer, mumble, growl, and holler clumsy English versions of their perfect Latin Mass, and do it at a priest staring them right in the face, and that in time all would be forced to clasp their neighbors' sweaty paws as part of the ritual, they would have told you that you had confused the Church with the Rotary, or maybe the Kiwanis. And if you had insisted that indeed, there was still more, and said that the Epistles and the Gospels would be read not only in our native tongue, but by laymen, they would have either roared in helpless laughter, or else had you committed. Only a person who had taken leave of his senses could have dreamed up such a thing. It was Protestants who did those things. They were Catholics, and they knew which was better.

I cannot for the life of me square the way they thought and acted about their religion in their home and in their Church with the way they thought and acted about religion outside of those two places. I believe it was F. Scott Fitzgerald who said that the first-rate mind is one enabling its possessor to hold two contradictory ideas at the same time. If he was right, Charlie and John had exemplary first-rate minds. Each of them was solemnly and unalterably convinced that everybody—Catholics and renegades (their term for lapsed Catholics who formally became Protestants and were held to be especially treacherous; Catholics who merely quit going to church were "fallen away," and there was some skeptical hope for them), Protestants from birth,

Jews, Muslims, Buddhists—*everybody* knew that the Holy Roman Catholic Church was the best and only faith. The others, all ersatz, therefore were always out to get us, so we'd better be on our toes.

There was never just one reason to explain why some non-Catholic third party had caused, connived, or colluded in any decision disappointing a Catholic. There was always another one, and it always came first. If a professionally incompetent fellow communicant was denied a job promotion in an operation managed by Protestants, the main reason was that he was a Catholic. If a bumptious, irascible, stupid, and generally intolerable jerk was rebuffed in his application to join a country club, and he was a Catholic, that proved the club's stated nonsectarian policy was a palpable fraud. Every presidential election year made them angry again about what had happened to Al Smith in 1928.

I realize that they in those years right after World War II had personal memories of the Know-Nothings, and the KKK, and the NINA signs ("No Irish Need Apply"), and I know that Charlie never would have been elected to his town offices had not he and his enterprising coreligionists welded their number together into a small but efficient voting machine that monolithically voted for Catholic candidates and was equipped with some sort of smeller to discriminate in purely Protestant contests between "friend of ours—he's all right" and "lousy, rotten bigot." But I also know that Doris, though she converted to the Church before John married her in it, was a Protestant. I know that Charlie had arranged election of Protestants to the Board of Directors; they must have decently ratified his mercies to those borrowers and made them just as much their own—besides, who had ready cash in those days to buy up foreclosed properties? Good sense as well as decency was involved in the matter, too. Among those men was Carl Burrell, from whom John purchased the blue '50 Olds 98 coupe, which succeeded the trouble-plagued green torpedo, the lovely '53 Holiday that I polished down to metal, his own '57 bronze and beige 98 Holiday coupe, my mother's '61 metallic blue, Super 88 coupe, my cousin Emily's '62 black Super 88 sedan, and the car that survived him, the '62 maroon Holiday. There were at least three Catholic families running automobile dealerships in Rockland and nearby in those days, and those were major purchases, but John dealt with the pagan dealer. In the late Fifties, when he wavered between staying on at Rockland High until retirement at sixty-five (thus reigning over the new building he had been instrumental in promoting and then building, rolling over opposition like some genial juggernaut) and bowing to the obvious fact that the treasurership of the Massachusetts Teachers Association had become a full-time job, no longer manageable on nights and weekends, the trusted adviser and confidante who convinced him to take early retirement as headmaster and labor in Boston for the MTA was its executive secretary, Hugh M. Nixon, droll and smart as he could be, but still a Protestant. No, it can't be done; there is no way to reconcile what they said and what they did with what they said and what they did, not where religion was concerned.

And it doesn't matter much now, I guess, except as mental exercise. What matters now is not how the eccentric flywheel spun, or what on earth possessed me to start buying British sports cars—a Triumph TR-3, and then a TR-4, and after that a Sunbeam Alpine; John had been dead for six long years when I applied the lessons he had taught me about car haggling to buying my first Jaguar XK-E—when I knew he hated them (he said they weren't reliable, and as usual, he was quite right) or what possessed him, hating them, to give me money for them.

Attention, ladies and gentleman. Here are the starting lineups for today's game.

What matters now is not that as much as we did love

each other, we did have our differences. I finally got my hands on that red and gray Holiday in 1957, early in the spring of my senior year, and seeing no need of upsetting John, installed with the help of some of my baseball-playing friends a nifty hidden cut-out switch that bypassed the muffler at the manifold connection, reconnecting with the tailpipe farther aft. John made no strong objection when he saw the chrome downspout that bounced the sound waves off the pavement, and I never used that neat device when he was within earshot, but when he wasn't I got more than full use out of it—Kathie thought it was just great. Came then that fine Saturday spring evening, and I'd waxed that car to gleaming, and I picked her up to see a movie in Brockton. The traffic light at the intersection of West Water Street and Plain Street halted us. I hit the bypass switch and shifted the Hydramatic into Neutral. I knew that light, I'd timed it lots, in the sluggish blue sedan, and just before it changed I stuck the pedal in the firewall so that big vee-eight was roaring when the green signal came on and I slapped it into L (Low).

I suppose I left about a thousand miles or so of Goodrich Supercushion whitewall tire tread smoking on the pavement as that car hunkered down and then jumped off the line (and tires were not as good then—ten or twelve thousand careful miles was about all you ask for from a forty-dollar low pressure bias-ply, so that performance had cost eight bucks— four dollars off each rear tire—just getting underway). I think the speed limit was thirty miles per hour on that stretch of West Water Street, but it may have been twenty—not that it really matters: I was well over it, in Super, creating about as much noise as one of Claire Chennault's P–40 Flying Tigers, when I passed the tall bushes at Estes Auto Supply that concealed not only the eastern side of its parking lot that night but Sergeant Fred Damon of the Rockland Police, in his well-kept cruiser. He proceeded smartly out of the lot as we went by, but he didn't have to give chase; I stopped at the brook about two hundred yards down and unwillingly reviewed in my mind the private penalties established at 457 Union Street for moving violations: all fines and fees, together with any resulting insurance surcharges, to be discharged in their entirety from the personal funds, or expectations thereof, of the operator (just like stupid bets on play-off games with Galehouse pitching); an additional penalty of grounding for one week for each five miles per hour in excess of posted speed limit, recorded on citation by arresting officer. (There was a bit of paternal hypocrisy there: John drove like a bat out of hell. The Hingham High School kids called the '50 coupe "the blue bomber," and I was in the car with him when he met several members of the Massachusetts State Police, as well as one or two troopers each in Pennsylvania, Connecticut, New York, New Jersey, Maryland, and Delaware.) I seem to recall calculating rapidly that if Freddie would only be content to write me up for forty or so, I might still stand a chance of getting the wheels back in time for the prom. By the time I got home from the movie, I might even be able to think up some plausible mitigating story to diminish my crime.

Things turned out quite badly. Freddie cordially spurned my license and the registration. "No, no, George," he said, "I know who you are, and I know who owns the car. Where the hell you think you're going?" I told him, once I got enough moisture in my throat. A small hope lighted in my mind: perhaps Freddie was going to let me off with a warning. All I would have to do was promise never, ever, ever to pull that stunt again, and perhaps brown-nose myself into complete degradation, but anything would be better than grounding. "Well, that's nice," Freddie said, "but you were going too fast, and you should get that muffler fixed, too." I guess I probably nodded. He straightened up and stepped back from the Olds. The small hope was now a bright flame.

"You're not," I said, very humbly, "you're not going to give me a ticket?"

"Of course not," he said, "no need to do that. I'm just going to call up your father. You just go along to the movie now. I'm sure you won't do it again."

John told me—after the movie, which I had not enjoyed at all—that the only reason he was suspending all but two weeks of the sentence to grounding was Fred Damon's interposition of a plea for leniency when he heard what John's personal ordinance called for.

Leading off, and playing center field: DiMaggio. Di-Maggio, playing center field.

What matters now are other things. Although he had a personality more authoritative than he needed, when the time came for what should have been commencement of his gradual cession of responsibility for the child to the young man I had become; and although I chafed under his benevolent domination probably much longer than I should have (make no mistake about this: John never once hit me, but I was scared of him. All he had to do to destroy me was say: "George, I'm disappointed. I didn't expect this from you."); those were just our errors. There were others, worse, and most of those were mine. When I finally realized that I had no choice but to assert some independence, I thought that nothing short of a whole continent of distance would make the point for me (he was terribly hurt, making the understandable if exaggerated inference that more than an ordinary need for adult autonomy was meant; he thought I didn't like him, and that I had repudiated everything he stood for when I went to Stanford Graduate School. He became so desperate that he tried to bribe me to stay in New England for grad school; he offered to buy me a Corvette, that he

208

could not afford, if I would stick to home. I dismissed that offer out of hand, concealing my incipient panic: he was getting close to my price, and if he had upped it to one of those new E-type Jags—silver, say?—I would have folded like a napkin. I even made things worse: I said that when I got the Ph.D. I never got, I intended to work and live in the West—shows you how confidently important choices can be made when you have no facts for their bases). But the damage wasn't total; both of us were suitably chastened by my self-imposed year's exile, and thereafter very peaceably resumed sharing the few years we had for that. In retrospect it seems a funny thing: John treated me as an adult every day of my life until the one when he detected signs I'd started to become one. I think he got scared, too. There wasn't any other kid around the house that I saw; I guess he was scared of me. Baseball's not the only simple game that's very hard to play.

Batting second, playing shortstop: Pesky. Pesky, playing shortstop.

He told me after Charlie's death, when Doris, he, and I had regained some equilibrium, that burying his father was the hardest thing he'd done and he hadn't done it well. I thought he'd done it very well, and I told him that. He shook his head and said no, and then he said he'd always known he'd really never measured up to the man that Charlie'd been, and the funeral proved it to him. I sincerely— and correctly—disputed that, and I told him that no one could possibly have shown a stronger mettle under sorrow. He did not believe me then, although he said he did, nor did he believe me when he talked about it later, when something had not gone right, but "would have if Pa'd been here. He would have known just what to do."

I do not think when he said those things that he was consciously preparing me for the way that I would feel only eleven brief years later, after Doris and I buried him. I do not think he spoke those words intentionally planning to leave behind not only all his worldly goods and an empty chair at the head of the table, but also some reassurance should I feel I'd let him down. But intended or not, that was still the effect of those things he said. When the time came, and passed, I did think that I'd let him down, and never had quite measured up to the standard that he met, even when we buried him, and that if I'd been the man he was, or if he'd been around to do it, things would have been done right. Then I remembered what he told me, and I felt somewhat consoled.

Batting third, and playing left field: Williams. Williams, playing left field.

I think Saint Nicholas was still delivering and decorating the Christmas tree the year I got the Lionel Santa Fe red-and-silver double-diesel locomotives. The rolling stock included the black hopper car that dumped the coal into the bin of the loader with the continuous black rubber conveyor belt that scooped up the coal and dropped it down to refill the hopper car. There was also the cattle car with rubber black and white steers that had little feelers on their hooves; when the train stopped at precisely the right place opposite their motorized platform corral, they sometimes actually emerged from their transport, vibrating along on their feelers and lining up in the stalls until the train came by again and we opened up the gates and jiggered them back into the car— most times they got stuck either entering or leaving the car, and had to be unstuck with a deus ex machina forefinger. It's possible, though, that Santa didn't really bring that train; it replaced the cast-iron American Flyer Blue Streak locomotive and uninteresting cars I had gotten from him several Christmases before, during the war, when I was barely old enough to play with it and so dropped and cracked it several times; by the time the first Lionels arrived, Charlie may have been springing for the loot, while I humored him and John by crediting Saint Nick. I know that later when I got the silver Union Pacific double diesels with the silver streamlined cars—one of them was Vista-domed—Santa had been retired, and I thanked the persons actually responsible for enabling me at last to use my flashy Santa Fe locomotives for the passenger hauls—not freight—the real railroad used them for (the A.T. & S.F. had dowdy old engines to pull real cattle cars and coal cars). The Union Pacific engines were freight haulers, and it was a satisfying swap.

Charlie had George Skillings and his son build me a great table out of gypsum board down cellar, so big that when we moved out of Pacific Street and into Charlie's house after he died in '55, the table had to be cut in half to get it through the bulkheads. I became a manager of the Rockland High basketball team soon after that train layout was complete, with tunnels through a big papier mâché mountain at the northeast corner, the White Sands missile testing ground at the southeast corner, brooks bridged over by culverts on both sides of the town of lighted buildings and lawns (in winter, snowed) that sprawled between the southwest and the northwest corners. There the cattle did their routines, and the coal went on and off, and the Super Chief delivered and collected passengers for its next trip. All of this was controlled by the big ZF transformer, whistles blowing, engines backing, trains emerging from the tunnel on tracks different from the ones on which they'd entered. (I had remote switches in there; all visitors dutifully pronounced themselves amazed.) Many nights when there were basketball games, I got home after John returned from Hingham, and I would find him down there in the cellar, sitting at the transformer, playing with what by then I knew were not just *my* trains. That was okay, though, because I had discovered girls, and although I had not been able to acquire any firsthand information, as it were, surmised that they would be even more fun to play with than trains. John divined this, and silently disapproved, at least partly because he wanted me to be there when he was the engineer.

He was also home, as I recall, on September 28th of 1960, six years and one day before he died (that day in '60 was a Wednesday—he must have had a cold), when Pete Blewett and I, for no particular good reason, came back to my house and John had the ball game on. We sprawled on the floor in front of his chair and propped our chins in our hands to watch the seventh-place Red Sox (65–89, .422) play their last home game of the season in Motorola ten-inch black and white. We saw the gray image of Ted Williams hit homer 521, the last of his career in his last time at bat (he'd announced retirement plans), in the indistinct white speck disappearing into the bleachers in right field, and John said: "Well, that's the end of something."

John never felt great warmth for Williams; like Charlie, he believed in making demands quite impossible even for a superstar to meet, and when they went unsatisfied, he downgraded the man. Nevertheless, he did not welcome Ted's last time at bat, and in the six years that John watched of Carl Yastrzemski's twenty-three-year run, he didn't come to like Yaz either. He wanted Ted to play again. More than he mistrusted Williams, John mistrusted change.

Of course he died the year before Yaz played an entire season like a man possessed, and the Red Sox won the pennant. That might have mollified John somewhat, at least until the seventh game of the Series against the Cardinals, when Yaz's blend of luck and drive finally fell short in a dying foul pop-up to third, with the man with the tying run standing almost under it, watching helplessly as the soaring season slowly fell at last to earth.

Playing first base, and batting fourth: York. York, playing first base.

The students in John's English classes at Natick and Hingham high schools were always giving him things. A girl in Natick gave him a gray-and-white puppy we named Gyp. We had no idea how valuable a purebred Siberian husky was, but somebody else (we suspected the milkman) did: Gyp disappeared, and no trace of him was found. When John taught at Hingham High he had a student named Rosemary Denmark who became so caught up in his classes that she applied no inconsiderable talent and effort at calligraphy to illuminate on parchment the last lines of William Cullen Bryant's poem "Thanatopsis." John had it framed and positioned it so that as you descended the four steps from the second floor to the first landing in the hall of the house on Union Street, it was right before your eyes. Many times I caught him pausing there in the morning, and I do not think he was looking at all the holy pictures in gilt frames surrounding it. I think he was regretting the teaching days behind him, and looking forward to the day when he would retire again, this time early from the MTA, and activate arrangements he had made to teach English at Stonehill College. A trip to Ireland was planned, too; his first adventure, and also Doris's, taking place where Charlie called "across the water." Sixty-two was his target birthday to embark on those delights. He was sixty when he died.

That was far too soon, but fully in conformity to Cullen Bryant's stricture. John had so lived that when his summons came to join the innumerable caravan that travels in the silent halls of death, he went not like the galley slave, scourged to his dungeon, but as one who wrapped the drapery of his couch about him, and lay down to pleasant dreams.

It really is too bad, though, that he never saw Susan and John, and that he and Charlie and his grandson John and I cannot now meet at Gate A of a summer's gentle evening and find our way again, all together for just once, among the maze of concrete ramps that do really go someplace, emerging at what seems like long last into tinted evening, the great green Wall out there in left, the grass meticulously mowed, the young men with idle swagger working out muscle kinks, and take our appointed seats to wait for that gravel voice requesting our attention. The Stage Manager gave us the latitude and longitude, but He did not divulge His telephone area code and number. If I had them, I would call Him up and ask whether the two of them might have a furlough like Emily did when she went back to see the Town once more. I would assure Him that this one would have happier consequences. John and Charlie would not come back chagrined and disappointed, not the way she did, because my son John and I have everything all planned, and this will be a good time.

I'd think the two of them could handle it all right. *Leading off, and playing center field: Burks. Burks, leading off and playing center field.* It would take them some time to adjust. They would want to know where the hell DiMaggio went. But John would be eighty-three this May, old enough to adapt, and Charlie at a baseball game never lost his temper at anyone but Boston's players.

Batting second, and playing second base: Barrett. Barrett, playing second base and batting second. Charlie might have some trouble getting used to that, as good as Barrett is; Charlie would want Bobby Doerr. I do like Marty Barrett, but for that one occasion, having worked it out beforehand with my son, at home, I think I would side with Charlie. My father, to be contrary, would ally with my son John, if for no other reason than the sameness of their names, just as my son and I had planned it, and the battle would be joined.

I suppose the Stage Manager might be a bit incredulous. "Wait a minute," He would say, "Do you know Who you're talking to? Just what is it you think you want these guys let out of? It's not the other place, you know—this is Heaven, all right, pal? Have you got that straight? We've got all the best times here. You should read the Book, I think, which come to think of it I've been meaning to get in touch with you for some time anyway—you could use improvement there."

I would try to placate Him. I would be respectful. I would say: "Look, I know this, and I mean no offense. I heard You run a classy joint, very highly recommended. But Fenway Park's not up there, see? And it's nothing personal, You know, nothing against You. It's just that I know these guys. I grew up with them. I've known them all my life. We had some good times together. And the best times that we ever had were the ones at Fenway Park."

I think the Manager might go for that. Especially when I finished up: "Okay, just go and ask them. Just see if they want to come. Tell them this is Next Year, this really is the year. This is the year the Red Sox win the Series."

"You're sure of that?" the Manager would say.

"Absolutely sure," I'd say. "Copper-bottomed, ironclad, absolutely sure." And then I'd hit him with the clincher. "Look," I'd say, "I can get an extra ticket. Why don't You come down with them, take in a game Yourself. Nice spring night, Clemens going, should be a good one." That would do it, I am sure, and maybe that is all He's wanted, all those years He's stayed away: not just all those desperation calls, screamed from the stands and at TVs all around New England with two out and a run down in the home half of the ninth, in a last-ditch game, but a good seat on the first-base line that would give Him a real stake in what goes on at Fenway Park, on this blessed earth. Then He might understand.

In 1918 . . . the last time.

ACKNOWLEDGMENTS

E ver since I started out in the newspaper business, I have been time and time again amazed by the eagerness of people to talk about the way they make their livings. The cops in Warwick, Rhode Island, were generous with their time to a cub reporter, as were the firemen and the school officials. When I went to Springfield, Massachusetts, for the Associated Press, Mayor Charles Ryan and his City Councilors were just as gracious as the officers and men that I met at Westover Air Force Base. When a series of organized crime trials (they weren't called that in those days—"Mafia" was still in official usage) began in the Hampden County Courthouse, the clerks and the judges and the lawyers were all as helpful as they possibly could be, and played a large part in my decision to go to law school. State Police, F.B.I. agents, the friends I made in what was then the Treasury Department's Alcohol, Tobacco and Firearms Division (it's since been absorbed into the bureau), more lawyers, judges, clerks, and some garrulous hoods as well: all of them seemed to like nothing better than to sit and talk for hours with a young man who didn't know a blasted thing, but who was interested. I think now, after many conversations with nice people who have read my books, that I have the explanation: everyone's a storyteller, or would like to be if time permitted—just as I would like to have been a major league ballplayer, if time, and ability, had permitted.

In the course of the years I have bothered a lot of people, some of them politicians elected to high office—and boy, that simple game is hard to play—and many others appointed to high stations. I have cross-examined hired killers, who really didn't like me and who certainly had the power to do something about it, and antagonized some judges, and almost everywhere I've met with cordiality. Never have I been so scared to ask for an interview as I was when I bothered Ted Williams while he was heckling Rich Gedman at the batting cage in Winter Haven. I took up half of Dick Radatz's working day. I think Dominic DiMaggio gave me about three hours of one of his, and Ted Lepcio spent most of an evening with me. When Bobby Doerr was in Cooperstown, New York, for his induction into the Hall of Fame, he gave me almost an hour of his tightly scheduled time, and when I talked to Johnny Pesky in Florida, well, no one could have been more gracious. Jim Lonborg let me take a chunk out of a family Sunday afternoon, and was as patient in the New England winter of 1988 as he had been a quarter-century before in the Red Sox clubhouse after an especially tough loss, when my AP duties obliged me to ask him to account for the shellacking he had taken: "Some nights," he said, "some nights you're just not breaking off the curve," a compact piece of wisdom usefully to be recalled by the writer in his own work, on the days when it won't go right. So I thank each of those men, along with Dick Bresciani, Josh Spofford, Jim Samia, Debbie Matson, and especially Mary Jane Ryan in the Red Sox press office; and Vince Doria, sports editor at the *Globe*, and his assistant, Nancy Curley, for fielding my more arcane queries (the *Boston Herald* is not listed here as a source; that is not because the *Herald* does not perform well on the daily sports beat in Boston—it does, and I miss Tim Horgan's columns—but because I have what appears to be an irreconcilable lexical dispute with the *Herald*'s circulation department: its managers evidently consider that a "morning newspaper" is one that exists in time for delivery before one P.M., while I with equal firmness hold that a "morning newspaper" is one which is delivered to the subscriber before eight A.M. on weekdays and nine A.M. on Sundays). Dick Johnson of the New England Sports Museum was eager to offer valuable archival help. There was much in this project for me, but nothing at all for those people except perhaps the small pleasures of talking about baseball with a fellow addict. Pete Palmer's contribution to my course of instruction is evident, I think, but my appreciation may not be, so I state it here.

There are several players whom I would have liked to talk to, but they are gone. Billy Goodman, Jackie Jensen, Ellis Kinder, to name a few: it was such a pleasure to watch them. I couldn't locate Clyde Vollmer, and I never did connect with George Kell or Carlton Fisk.

I interviewed only players who've retired, because what interested me was how the game has changed, and they have the necessary perspective. I interviewed only men who played at Fenway Park, because I thought, and still think, that the game is different there from what it is elsewhere. It's too big for a lodge meeting, too small for a ballgame, too hard to park near, and the food's terrible. But the view's beautiful and the suspense never ending—except, of course, in despair.

There are some omissions from this book; I made them deliberately. The Red Sox who captured me, and the management that employed them, in the middle Forties came from a milieu that inculcated, and enforced, a social and political vision quite different from the one that we Americans at least now officially endorse, and from time to time at least struggle to make real. In recent years there have been distressingly numerous and depressingly ugly reports, most of them too credible to disregard, that the racial bias that barred Jackie Robinson from the post-war Red Sox roster was but one—though the most prominent—exemplar of a bigotry inclusive of ethnic and religious strains as well, sufficiently pervasive as to corrode off-field relationships among players, and those between players and management. But the prevalence of those poisons was not confined in those days to the management suites of the Boston American League Baseball Company—Charlie and John, after all, did not fantasize all the evidence they educed to support their abiding if anomalous resentments of anti-Catholic bias, however they may have exaggerated or misinterpreted the proofs they had; neither of them acquired his mind-set from experience playing big-league ball. And if the toxins have lingered in baseball well after their perniciousness has been identified and denounced, well, there are pockets of viciousness yet virulent today in society at large. The microcosm available for viewing on the other side of the turnstiles is a more orderly and usually more entertaining one than the macrocosm that surrounds the great lawn and the flat green Wall, but the people who work in it come from the same raucous, sometimes mean, society that provides the people who come to watch them, and they are imperfect, too. I do not pay my way into Fenway Park in order to subject myself to an uplifting and morally improving spirtual experience, whether as a result of exhortation or display of saintliness; I go there to watch talented athletes play baseball, and if off the field they and their employers commit a variety of socially disapproved high crimes and misdemeanors, that is their affair. When I get ready to write a book detailing all my sins, I will start making notes as well for a sequel setting down all the offenses they committed when they were not playing ball. Realists may wish to open a new file: "Two books we don't expect to see very soon."

One last acknowledgment: In more than forty years I have watched, admired, and ached with lots of ballplayers who wore Red Sox uniforms but whose names did not come up here. Norm Zauchin, for example (Ted Lepcio called my attention to this): his '55 rookie season at first base yielded figures (.239, 27 homers, 93 RBI's) superior to those put up by Mickey Mantle in his '51 debut with the Yankees (.267, 13 homers, 65 RBI's—and if you want to say that Mantle's ninety-six games that year didn't afford him as many opportunities to shine as Zauchin got in his 130 outings four years later, here is what Mantle did in 142 games in 1952: .311, 23 homers, 87 RBI's). Zauchin and the likes of Grady Hatton, Billy Klaus, Gene Stephens, and Sammy White, a whole parade of strivers, came and went across the stage at Fenway to my delight. So for all the men who played there, even those I never saw: you gave me a lot of good times, and I thank you very much.

G. V. H.

INDEX OF NAMES
AND ASSOCIATIONS

Page numbers in italics are keyed to photographs.

Nixon, Hugh M., 205
Nixon, Russ, 44

Oakland A's, 38, 58, 98–99, 100,
   101, 104, 105, 121, 151, 153,
   159, 188
O'Hara, John, 29
Ojeda, Bobby, 105
O'Neill, Gerry, 51–52
O'Neill, Steve, 44–45
O'Neill, Thomas P. ("Tip"), Jr.,
   115
O'Reilly, Terry, 180
Orlando, Johnny, 86, 89
Orr, Bobby, 10, 78, 131, 179
Osterman, John, 194
Owen, Spike, 109, 157, 187

Pagliarulo, Mike, 182
Palingo, Joe, 182
Palmer, Pete, 61–62, 77, 99,
   102–3, 116–17, 149, 151,
   152
Parish, Robert, 180
Parnell, Mel, 188
Perez, Tony, 84
Pesky, Johnny, 42, 45, 75
   hitting by, 8, 11, 141
   as manager, 41
   opinions of, 25, 61, 63, 64, 71,
   79, 109–12, 145
Petrocelli, Rico, 71, 126
Philadelphia Athletics, 7–8, 118
Philadelphia Phillies, 39, 60, 123
Piersall, Jimmy, 141
Pittsburgh Pirates, 115
Pizzarro, Juan, 124
Putnam, Hugh, 142

Radatz, Dick, 50–51, 56, 146
   hitting by, 24

opinions of, 44, 54, 61, 64, 66,
   70, 71, 169, 187
as pitcher, 43, 48, 59–60
Reed, Jody, 187
Remy, Jerry, 68, 69, 129
Rhodes, Dusty, 104
Rice, Jim, 70, 173–74, 181
   fielding by, 34, 68, 107–8, 144,
   169
   hitting by, 55, 90–92, 128,
   143, 150–51, 157–58, 165–
   66
   record of, 61, 62, 69, 80
   vision problem of, 107–8
Rinkus, Jack, 138, 146, 148
Ripkin, Cal, Jr., 93
Romine, Kevin, 143
Romo, Vicente, 124, 125
Runnels, Pete, 120, 164, 165
Russell, Bill, 10
Russell, Rip, 11
Ruth, Babe, 62

St. Louis Browns, 37, 118
St. Louis Cardinals, 29, 38, 99,
   103, 104, 119–20, 123, 212
San Francisco Giants, 106
Schilling, Chuck, 44
Schiraldi, Calvin, 105–6
Schroeder, Jay, 77
Score, Herb, 170
Scott, George, 126, 128
Seattle Mariners, 60, 101, 128
Seattle Pilots, 121, 128
Sellers, Jeff, 57, 144, 166–67
Shore, Eddie, 10
Siebert, Sonny, 124, 125
Skillings, George, 211
Smith, Lee, 106, 109, 144, 186
Smith, Reggie, 126
Society of American Baseball Re-
   search (SABR), 62